HOW to PUNT, PASS and KICK

Random House   New York

HOW to PUNT, PASS and KICK

BY RICHARD PICKENS
Drawings by Fran Chauncy

This title was originally catalogued by the Library of Congress as follows:

Pickens, Richard.
How to punt, pass, and kick. Drawings by Fran Chauncy.
New York, Random House ₁1965₁
xiii, 173 p. illus. 22 cm. (The Punt, pass, and kick library, 1)

1. Kicking (Football) 2. Passing (Football) 3. National Football
League. I. Title.

GV951.5.P5   796.3322   65—22657

Library of Congress   ₁65l14₁

Trade Ed.: ISBN: 0-394-80191-1   Lib. Ed.: ISBN: 0- 394-90191-6

Contents

Introduction

This book has been written to teach boys how to play football. All the instruction material comes from expert authorities: coaches and players of the NFL. Their advice, guidance, and warnings are based on years of experience in the greatest football league in the world.

They believe that you must begin your football career with a solid foundation: good playing habits and willingness to practice long hours to develop the game's basic skills—until you *automatically* make every play in the proper manner.

There is no way to avoid getting bumped and bruised in the game of football. There is no guarantee that a boy who plays the game will never get hurt. But the chance of serious injury can be greatly reduced by following the safety precautions recommended in this book. If safe, correct methods of play become a habit at an early age, then you will greatly increase your chances of avoiding injury and becoming an outstanding player.

The safest and most sensible approach to football is to learn ow to perform the five fundamentals of the game: blocking, tackling, passing, punting, and place kicking. In addition, you should learn how to play every position on the field—from offensive guard to defensive halfback, from middle linebacker to center. Even though you won't play most of the positions at which you will gain experience, the knowledge will increase your understanding of the game. You will be able to *think good football* automatically on the playing field.

This book offers you the same principles of instruction as those used by coaches in the NFL. Besides the game's basic skills, you will learn how to use your body weight in tackling and blocking, how to approach an opponent, and even how to fall properly to the ground. You will also understand the importance of body balance and learn the common mistakes to avoid.

Of course there is a difference between football played by boys and the game as played by professionals. In the NFL every man is a specialist, playing in just one position—either on offense or defense. Some men earn their salary just by punting or place kicking. The NFL teams use complex offensive plays and tricky defensive formations.

The game played by schoolboys is much simpler. In this book you will be learning *basic lessons* and *correct techniques* of football just as it is played in the NFL. But the job of teaching you specific plays is up to your coach. Every coach uses his own choice of plays, and makes changes in the basic T formation as he sees fit.

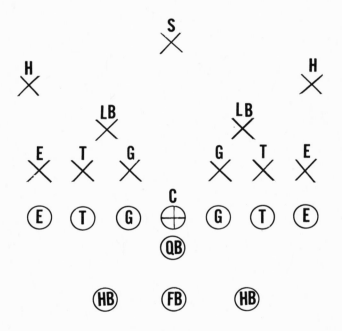

The coach of every school team will have to devise his own plan of attack, for such teams vary greatly—both in the number of boys trying out for the team, and in the ability of the players. A coach must use the *natural strength* he can find in his own players. He may have to build his attack around his best back—whether the player is a passing quarterback or a power-running fullback. Depending on where the coach positions his best linemen, he may have to run eighty percent of all plays to the right or left side of the line.

In the NFL, where *every* player has great talent, it isn't necessary to concentrate on "playing your strength." Every team can offer a balanced attack, and no team has a real weak spot in either the line or backfield.

Many boys want to play football simply because they enjoy it. Others hope to continue playing in college, and some have the dream of playing in the NFL one day. But whatever your personal ambition, promise yourself to treat your body with the greatest possible care.

Dick Lane, outstanding defensive back of the Detroit Lions, is entering his fourteenth year in the NFL. Rarely injured, Dick is an excellent example of a player who has lasted a long time in a bruising contact sport, while playing at a peak of efficiency every minute he is on the field. Dick has the following good advice for young players:

Make up your mind to play football using only the proper, safe techniques. Learn how to make a tackle and throw a block, and be sure you know how to fall to the ground after you have crashed into an opponent. Before you develop bad habits in passing, punting, or place kicking, learn how these skills are properly performed.

Remember at all times that football is a *thinking game*—not just a series of exercises in muscle and brawn. With the proper attitude, determination, and willingness to perfect your abilities by constant practice, you will be able to develop your skills to their fullest degree.

HOW to PUNT, PASS and KICK

1
Safety First

There are a few very important safety precautions which should be followed by every boy who plays football. They are based both on common sense and on the recommendation of every coach in the NFL.

Use Good Equipment

Always wear proper equipment, even during light practice sessions. A helmet is your most important piece of equipment, since it protects your head.

To fit properly, the inside webbing of a helmet should fit snugly onto your skull, yet still leave plenty of air space between the webbing and the helmet's outer shell. There must also be air space between your ears and the helmet.

A helmet that fits too tightly against any part of your head is dangerous because it cannot protect your head by absorbing the shock of direct impact.

A helmet that fits too loosely is also dangerous. It can be knocked off by a tackle or a block, leaving your head unprotected while a play is still going on. If a knee or a cleat strikes your head or face, while it is unprotected, you may be severely injured.

Do not borrow another boy's helmet. A helmet which fits poorly can be just as dangerous as wearing no helmet at all.

Wearing only part of your equipment is also flirting with danger. If you fail to wear shoulder pads, for instance, your shoulder can be wrenched or severely damaged. Even though such an injury cannot be fatal, it can be very painful. And it can end your football days at a very young age.

Ask your coach to help you make sure your equipment fits properly. The basic football equipment consists of:

Helmet
Shoulder pads
Long, tuck-in jersey
Trousers, with hip and thigh padding
Long, heavy socks
Cleats

Always Warm Up

At least five minutes of warming up should precede every practice or game. In very cold weather, you should begin warming up very gradually and exercise for a longer period than in warm weather, to make sure you "loosen" your entire body.

Begin a warm-up session with mild exercises such as running in place and bending from the waist. Then gradually enter into more strenuous calisthenics such as touching your toes and "squat jumps." Always make sure that your *entire body* has been limbered before engaging in physical contact.

A "cold" body is subject to strains and muscle pulls. Even though such injuries are minor, they often take weeks to heal.

Always Get a Physical Exam

Most schools require every student to have a physical examination at the start of a school year, either by the school doctor or by the family physician. Where this is not the practice, however, *it is vitally important that you get a thorough physical exam before running onto a football field.* Even if you have never been injured and feel in top condition, a physical exam may reveal something wrong with your body. Prompt medical attention will usually prevent such trouble from becoming serious.

5

Don't Try to be Tough

An obviously minor injury such as a bruised finger may be nothing to worry about. But any kind of pain —even a "funny feeling" in your body—should send you to a doctor.

Don't make the mistake of thinking that ignoring pain or an injury is being "tough."

Jim Kanicki, the great defensive tackle of the Cleveland Browns, weighs 270 pounds and is as hard as nails. But he goes to the team doctor with even a slight bruise—just to make sure his injury isn't serious. His coach, Blanton Collier, says:

> Jim is a smart athlete. He knows that playing while hurt, just to prove how tough you are, is foolish. For in doing so you may be cheating both yourself and your team. Even a minor injury may take a long time to heal. And the time a player spends sitting on the sidelines might have been prevented if he had seen a doctor when he first got hurt.
>
> Follow Jim's rule and see your school doctor as soon as you suffer an injury—no matter how small it seems to be.

Play with Boys Your Own Size and Age

A boy who weighs 80 pounds just isn't big enough to take the shock of tackling or blocking a player who weighs 120 pounds. At a weight difference of 40 pounds, the bigger boy is fifty percent heavier than the smaller player.

It's a different story in the NFL. A guard weighing 240 can safely hit a defensive tackle of 280 pounds —even though they have a similar weight difference of 40 pounds. For the bigger tackle is only 16 percent heavier than the smaller man.

A boy's body does not finish growing, or become "hardened," until he is in his twenties. His muscles aren't as tough as a grown man's and he can't take the same kind of beating. He'll be risking serious injury if he plays football against stronger and heavier boys.

Avoid Dangerous Playing Areas

Many boys have been injured on hard playgrounds or on poorly cared-for football fields in public parks. Many such injuries would never have happened on good playing fields.

Don't allow yourself to be talked into playing football on a hard-surfaced school or public playground. If such an area is the only one available in your neighborhood, play "touch" football. *And avoid all blocking and tackling.* The human body just isn't built to withstand the shock of hitting concrete or pavement.

If you intend to play in a public park or in an area you have never seen before, inspect the ground carefully. It may look smooth at first glance, but you may discover dangerous holes or ruts in the earth, as well as pieces of broken glass or jagged rocks covered by the grass.

If you suddenly step into a rut while running at full speed, you can easily break or badly sprain an ankle. A piece of glass or rock can inflict a serious wound on your face or on any other part of your body.

Play only on a safe, inspected field. If you want to play a game on weekends or when you are not near a good playing area, stick to "touch" football.

Learn Body Control

During every exciting play of every NFL game, hundreds of pounds of muscle and bone run at top speed, block with precision, and tackle savagely. Often the thud of bodies striking bodies can be heard in the stands.

Despite the speed and hard-hitting action, the players on the field are in complete control of their bodies. A center, knocked off his feet by two rushing blockers, knows how to hit the ground without getting hurt. A defensive back tackling a 240-pound fullback knows how to use his weight so that his body receives a minimum of shock.

Two important factors in body control are learning how to hit an opponent and knowing how to fall.

Pat Fischer, the great defensive back of the St. Louis Cardinals, weighs only 170 pounds. Yet he is considered one of the toughest tacklers in the NFL. Pat, who tackles men outweighing him by 70 pounds, has learned how to make hard body contact without getting hurt. His coach, Wally Lemm, has explained it as follows:

Boys often make the mistake of "tightening up" and hesitating the instant before they make a tackle or block. As a result, they sometimes get badly shaken up. But there is far less chance of getting hurt if you follow Pat's example and move at full speed into your opponent, whether you are hitting him or being hit. If you slow up, you give your opponent the advantage of body momentum. And *you* absorb most of the shock when contact is made. If you, too, are moving fast, the shock will be divided.

Pat moves quickly at all times, controlling his body (setting himself properly either to tackle or to block), and gliding right into body contact at good speed.

Pat also knows how to fall properly.

His secret in not getting hurt is to keep his body *loose* rather than brittle after the initial impact. He doesn't just go limp. He keeps his body *firm*, but once contact has been made he doesn't mentally re-

9

sist the fact that he's on his way to the ground. Instead, he relaxes.

Pat has learned that you must not stiffen your body when you fall, for the blow will only seem harder. Don't ever stick out a rigid arm or leg to break your fall. You can easily break a bone, or suffer a dislocated joint, if another player lands on you while your arm or leg is stiffly extended. Instead, keep your arms bent and close to your body. As you land, *roll* rather than hit with a thud.

Like many NFL players, Pat has practiced for hours to perfect the art of falling properly.

The proper techniques for playing each position, as well as for tackling and blocking, will be discussed later in the book. But the point to remember now is that only recommended techniques of play should be used. Practice good body control by using only the proper playing techniques. It is the best possible way to avoid injury.

Don't Try to Look Spectacular

Playing to please the fans is a bad mistake. Not only is it "show-off" football, but it leads to bad habits which prevent you from becoming a really good player. Two examples of bad practices are throwing yourself through the air to tackle or block, or crashing needlessly into an opponent who is many yards removed from the action of the play. This kind of reckless play is bound to result in injuries.

Although you may impress the fans by using wild, undisciplined methods of play, you will never fool your coach or your teammates.

Allie Sherman, coach of the New York Giants, has made the following points about Tom Scott, his veteran 220-pound linebacker.

There are faster linebackers and bigger linebackers than Tom. But none are better—even though many of them get a lot more publicity than Tom. Tom doesn't look spectacular on the field for the simple reason that he's such a great player. He blends his power, speed, and skill so smoothly that he makes the game look easy. In addition, his experience and intelligence help him "smell" enemy plays in advance.

As a result, he's almost always in the right place at the right time. A deadly tackler, Tom always brings his man down quickly and cleanly.

I've seen many linebackers caught out of position on plays which Tom would stop easily. As a result of being fooled, the other men must make "spectacular plays" to tackle an opponent or knock down a pass. The fans who cheer wildly don't realize that Tom would have made the same play look easy. Nor do the fans realize that where a "spectacular" tackle may stop a runner after a six-yard gain, Tom would have cut the runner down after only a two-yard advance.

Tom developed good football habits at an early age. He never gave in to the temptation of trying to capture the admiration of the fans, for he realized that such a desire would automatically lead to bad playing habits.

Tom is a great "team" player, and a perfect example for boys to follow. Like all great players in the NFL, he knows that he's playing for his team—not for the people sitting in the stands.

Remember That Football Is a Game

There is no better way to learn football than to study the methods and techniques of the players in the NFL.

Learn all you can from them: how to block, tackle, fake, and even how to *think* football. But don't make the mistake of taking the game too seriously—at least while you are still a boy.

Professional football players are tougher than you are. They are stronger, can take more punishment, can last longer, and can run farther and faster. Football is their *job*.

Your football hours take place after school and on weekends, on a *part-time* basis. Even though you may be in excellent condition, your body simply hasn't been trained to take a hard physical beating day after day, or to go at top speed until you are close to exhaustion.

Work at football as hard as you like, but enjoy it as a *sport*. Stop playing as soon as you begin to feel "used up." By quitting before you become exhausted, you will be saving a lot of strength for the next day. Then, instead of running onto the field tired and bruised, you will feel fresh and strong.

Stay Awake until the Whistle Blows

Don't make the serious mistake of thinking a play has ended just because the action is no longer taking place on your part of the field. If you have finished your assignment and are standing 50 or 60 yards away from an exciting play, don't become so fascinated that you become a "spectator."

Remember that you are a perfectly legal target for a block until the referee's whistle officially ends the play. If you are staring open-mouthed down the field, an excited opponent may decide to throw a hard block at you. Even though such a move can't do his team any good, and doesn't really make sense, he will be perfectly within his rights because blocks can be thrown all over the field as long as play is going on.

Always remain alert, even if you are far away from the football, and be ready to leap away from a sudden attack.

2
What Position Should You Play?

Analyze Yourself as an Athlete

The most important fact to consider in deciding what position you want to play is your body's size and structure.

As a young boy, you can't guess exactly how much you are going to weigh when you are fully grown, or just how tall you will be. Nor can you estimate your exact strength, speed, or level of muscular coördination and reflex action.

All you can do is to make a sensible guess about your future size and build. If you have big bones, and are larger and stronger than most boys your age,

15

you will probably develop into a large man. If you are slim, with small bones and a delicate frame, you probably won't become as large or as strong.

Common sense will tell you that a big, slow boy can't become a good end. A small boy might develop into an outstanding end, but he would be foolish to think of becoming a tackle or linebacker. Such extreme cases are fairly obvious. But boys with an average build will find it harder to decide what position to play because they have more choice.

They should take a sensible approach to playing football and develop those basic skills at which they show more than average ability—running, passing, blocking, tackling, or even punting and place kicking.

Even if they develop skills they will never use, they won't be wasting their time. For they will have increased their value as an all-round football player. And if they know the proper techniques of play they will have a larger understanding of the game.

Average-sized boys, however, must realize that their size may change by the time they are fully grown. Often, when boys enter their teens, their body structure suddenly changes. In just a single summer a boy may grow six inches, or become heavier and more solid. Or he may simply *stop* growing.

So remember that the expression "average-sized"

applies to you only as long as you *are* that size compared with boys your own age. If, as your body develops, you see that you are bigger or smaller than your friends, adjust your thinking—and concentrate on playing a position that "fits" your body.

YOUR ATTITUDE

Naturally the position you *want* to play is important to you. But your desire must be looked at realistically. A big, slow boy can't become a star halfback any more than a slim sprinter can become a guard.

But the sprinter *does* have a choice between becoming an end or a back. And the big, slow boy can choose between playing center or tackle.

Reading this book from cover to cover will help you to determine the position best suited to your abilities. Later on, the physical requirements for each position will be described carefully, in terms of body size, strength, speed, durability, and ability to take punishment.

Even if you are positive that you have the size and the skills necessary to play a certain position, try to keep your thinking *flexible*. Don't become so obsessed with the idea of playing center that it would be a crushing blow to learn you would make a far better guard.

If your coach switches you to a new position,

don't fight him. Be grateful for his advice and give it a try. He will probably be right, and you will find you can use your natural abilities far better in the position he suggests. Not only will this help you, but it will help your team—because you will be a more effective athlete.

George Halas, coach of the Chicago Bears, has commented on how J. C. Caroline was forced to switch positions when he entered the NFL.

J. C. came to the Bears from college with a wonderful reputation as a running back. From the first moment he put on a Bear uniform in practice, there was no doubt about his great running ability. He was fast, shifty, and tricky.

But our training camp was loaded with lots of good, young running backs. And many of them were bigger than J. C.—heavier boys with thick legs and torsos, who were a lot harder to knock off their feet. In the NFL, where runners have to bang heads with huge defensive linemen, these bigger backs were able to stand more consistent punishment than J. C.—and better able to keep their balance when hit by tacklers.

So we took advantage of J. C.'s great speed and switched him to defensive back. He made the adjustment like a duck taking to water. His 185 pounds were enough weight for him to make solid tackles without getting hurt, and his great speed let him keep up with fast pass receivers.

I'm convinced J. C. would have been just an ordinary running back in our league. But as a defensive back, he became a star almost overnight.

3
The Five Fundamentals
of Football

Before learning how to play any specific position, you must have a solid understanding of the game's five fundamentals: blocking, tackling, passing, punting, and place kicking. Trying to play football without knowing proper playing techniques would be like studying algebra without understanding simple addition.

Study every one of these five fundamentals carefully. They are the ABC's of football, and will increase not only your understanding of the game, but also your ability as an athlete.

Blocking

Blocking is the foundation of football. It is the basic "horsepower" behind every play in a game—whether it be a 2-yard plunge through the line or a 60-yard pass.

Many boys have a completely mistaken idea of what blocking really is. They think it is a matter of "knocking heads" with the man they are assigned to block. Unless they knock their opponent flat on his back they feel they have failed to do their job.

This is not the case at all. You would be amazed at how many excellent blocks are thrown during every NFL game—*without the blocked man even being knocked off his feet.*

The key purpose of blocking is to *eliminate* an opponent from a vital area of play—not to flatten him. The best method is to out-think your opponent. Use body balance and trickery—not brute force—to take him out of the play. Good blocking requires as much *technique* as any other skill in the game of football.

Tricking a 260-pound defensive tackle into charging away from the direction of a play is just as effective as knocking him down—and a lot easier. Often trickery is even *more* effective than knocking a man down. If he falls, you are liable to tumble with him. And if you are on the ground, you will lose your chance to throw another quick block at another opponent.

The secret to good blocking is simple: Instead of trying to "blast" your opponent with one great lunge, *keep him busy by hitting him again and again,* with short driving "bumps" to his body. If you hurl yourself at him in one great rush and he dodges you, then he will be free to rush past you.

A defensive lineman can't do two things at once. If you keep him involved in a struggle with you, you are doing your job—even if he is still on his feet and charging hard. To keep him concentrating on you, stay in front of him, hitting him again and again.

Always remember that a block is not a single move. It is a series of short "drives" into your opponent, which will keep him off balance and fully occupied with you.

A study of the most basic block—that of an offensive lineman against a defensive lineman playing opposite him—will teach you the basic fundamentals for any type of blocking.

BODY POSITION

To start off with a fast "charge," you must begin with a good stance. Place your body and feet so that you are *balanced.*

The following drawing shows the right position for a lineman just before a play begins:

23

Lean forward, with your feet planted apart, at a distance approximately equal to the width of your shoulders. Put part of your weight on your right arm, which is held firmly against the ground. (Planting your feet shoulder-width apart is only a general guide. Some men have short legs and long bodies. Others have long legs and short bodies. To find your best stance, experiment and ask your coach for help.)

You must strike a perfect balance between the weight placed on your arm and on your feet. Remember that defensive players are allowed to use their hands. It is perfectly legal for them to grab, shove, pull, or twist you off balance.

To acquire good balance, line up against a teammate. Have him try charging into you. If you topple backward, you are putting too much weight on your feet and not enough "forward" weight on your arm.

Have him suddenly pull you toward him. If you fall on your nose, you are putting too much weight on your arm and not enough on your legs.

You can also be knocked to either side. Many players unconsciously lean to one side, by putting more weight on one leg than the other.

The only true way of testing your stance is practice.

YOUR CHARGE

A good offensive lineman charges forward within a fraction of a second after the ball is snapped from the center. This gives him the advantage of more force, or driving power, than his opponent, especially if the defensive lineman is bigger.

Protect yourself when you throw a block. You probably won't get hurt if you protect your face and neck. (NFL coaches strongly recommend that all boys use helmets with bars across the face for maximum protection.)

Study the proper upright blocking stance. After coming out of a low starting position, rise up—while still leaning forward—to begin the "duel" with your opponent. You should hold your arms high when your bodies meet, so that you can knock

his arms away if he tries to grab you with his hands.

Half the battle in any close-range block is to keep the defensive player from getting a good grip on you or your uniform with his hands.

Your shoulders should be hunched up (forcing your shoulder pads high on your shoulders to protect your neck). Your head must be "locked" in position, by holding your neck, back muscles, and arms rigid. No matter how excellent your equipment, you can be shaken up by a blow to the head if your head sits limply on your shoulders.

Don't offer your head as a target. Keep your neck rigid and your shoulders high. And *always* wear a good helmet that fits perfectly.

Don't block your opponent with your head. Use only your arms and shoulders to make contact. Until a man reaches his full growth, his neck is one of the weakest parts of his body. NFL players can successfully "spear" opponents with their helmets, but only because they are fully grown men with "bulldog necks."

Carefully supervised exercises will develop your neck muscles, which are very important. (In boxing these neck muscles are called the "shock absorbers.") In *any* contact sport, a well-developed neck is a great advantage. A weak, scrawny neck on a good athlete is like a strong chain with one weak link.

In line play, blocking is best done by taking short, choppy, or "digging" steps. This keeps you in control of your body and prevents your lunging forward off balance. If you miss your first thrust at an opponent, you must maintain your balance in order to charge at him again.

You must maintain body control from the second the play starts until it is ended by the referee's whistle.

Charge into your opponent with your body leaning forward. If you are thrust back, maintain your position—leaning forward with your arms up and shoulders hunched—and "dig" into him again, using short, choppy steps. Even if he is stronger and bigger than you are, this kind of attack will at least delay his advance.

Remember that often during a single play a blocker must "bump and charge" his opponent as many as ten or twelve times. When you keep the pressure on your target by hitting him again and again you are *sustaining your block.*

Running plays and passing plays require different blocking techniques.

BLOCKING FOR RUNNING PLAYS

If you are trying to "open a hole" in the enemy line for a running back, you must block aggressively.

You must take short, choppy steps directly into your opponent as the play begins. Charge forward from your set position powerfully, so that you either move him out of the way or force him to "fight" you, so that he can't make a tackle.

If the play is to be run to your right, you will want to knock your opponent to the left. Hit him head on. Then quickly shift your body to your right, driving him to the left. If the play is to be run to your left, you will want to knock your opponent to the right. Again meet him head on—but quickly shift your weight to the left, driving him to the right.

AVOID A COMMON MISTAKE

Don't start your block by leaping to one side of your opponent in order to drive him toward the other side. If you do, he will instinctively react against your move, shifting his body exactly where you don't want him to go. In other words, you will "telegraph" your intention as soon as the ball is snapped.

Instead, start every block with a straight, direct charge at your man. *Shift your body quickly to one side of him only after you have made initial contact.*

BLOCKING FOR PASSING PLAYS

Protecting your passer requires a less aggressive block than opening a hole for a running back. The reason is simple: Since your opponent's assignment is to reach your quarterback, he must make the initial charge. This is different from a running play, in which *you* must strike first to eliminate the defensive lineman.

Your only job is to *keep the defender away* from the quarterback until the ball is in the air. Even if you gradually get forced back five or six yards, you will be doing your job by giving your passer time to spot a receiver and release the ball.

The next time you watch an NFL game, notice how often players are massed around the quarterback as he gets ready to throw the ball. Sometimes defensive linemen are within inches of him. But those few inches might as well be a mile if the pass is completed.

SPECIAL BLOCKS USED BY LINEMEN

The blocks discussed below are *team* plays which depend on one or more teammates working together. Not all school teams use such blocks, but learning how they work will increase your understanding of the game.

1. *The Trap Block*

The "trap" is used against a rushing defensive lineman who is big, strong, and aggressive. Too often he "runs over" the man trying to block him.

In order to trap-block him, you "allow" this defensive player to rush past his blocker, who makes a fake effort to stop him, and lets him charge past. As the defensive man crashes through the line, he is suddenly blocked from the *side* by another blocker he hasn't even seen. This man is usually a guard who "pulls out" of the line.

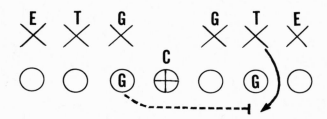

Hitting the onrushing defender from the side neutralizes his size and strength. Nine out of ten times a good trap block will knock the defensive man right out of the play. (Of course a lineman in the NFL will sense a trap coming if he finds it too easy to crash through the line.)

As used in the NFL, the trap block serves a good purpose. It keeps big defensive linemen on their toes. Once an experienced defensive end or tackle has crashed through the man blocking him, he will automatically hesitate and look to the side to make sure he isn't being trapped. This hesitation on the part of the defense helps the offense. Even a fraction of a second increases the chance of a play's making a big gain.

If an opposing team has a huge lineman who constantly breaks through his man, ruining play after play, the trap is the perfect weapon to slow him down.

2. *The Cross Block*

This block can easily be understood by looking at a simple diagram.

As you can see, two offensive linemen simply change assignments: Each slants toward the other's opponent. This move takes practice because it requires precise timing. Not only must each blocker know if he is to cross in front of or behind his teammate, but the move must be practiced again and again so they don't bump into each other. That would allow the two defensive linemen free passage into their backfield.

The cross block is an excellent weapon to surprise charging defensive linemen. By striking two big opponents from an unexpected angle, you destroy much of their "straight-ahead" power.

3. The Double-Team Block

This block, in which two men combine to block a single opponent, is so simple that even small boys can use it. It is most effective when short yardage is needed, and when the defensive end or tackle who is in a position to stop the play is a tough opponent.

If a running play is heading around right end, for instance, and only a couple of yards are needed for a first down, it makes good sense to "double team" the defensive end. This greatly increases the chance of the runner's making the needed two yards. However, it also decreases the chance of his making a long gain because one of the two blockers who have hit the end has given up the chance to hit the linebacker playing behind that end. This leaves the linebacker free to make the tackle after a short gain.

4. Downfield Blocking

Downfield blocking takes place beyond the line of scrimmage—often in an open field where players are running at full speed. During a game, each player on a team will probably make several downfield blocks.

Unlike blocking in line play, where each man has a specific assignment, downfield blocking requires that he *think on his feet*. Often he has only a second to make a move or to decide which of several players he should block.

Blocking beyond the line of scrimmage is a matter of "fencing" with the man who is your target. Rather than trying to knock him flat, you should concentrate on *forcing him away from the ball carrier*.

The objective is to place your body *between* your opponent and the ball carrier so that your opponent is forced to run *around* you, thereby losing valuable steps in his race to catch the runner.

Think of downfield blocking as a skilled duel with an opponent. Your weapons are trickery and the anticipation of his moves.

The following diagrams show the right and wrong way to make a downfield block on a defensive player while attempting to protect a runner.

The first method of attack is wrong. The blocker mistakenly commits himself (makes a strong, aggressive move) toward the defender. Unless he knocks the man down, the defender will probably be free to make the tackle.

R = Runner
B = Blocker
D = Defender

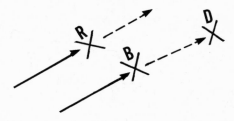

In the second diagram, the blocker is making a smart move. He is putting himself *between* the defender and the runner, and staying there. If the defender is faster than the blocker, he may eventually be able to run around him. But if the blocker keeps his body ahead of the defender, the defender must cut *behind* the blocker to get free. This will make the defender lose valuable yards in his efforts to catch the runner.

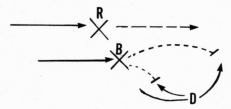

Even a *slow* lineman blocking a fast defensive back can delay the defender's approach to the ball carrier by using his body intelligently during a running "duel" with the defender.

Coördination, practice, body control, and timing can make up for a lack of strength, speed, and size in any kind of blocking. If you become a good blocker, you will have mastered the most basic playing technique in football. In addition, you will increase your value to your team—no matter what position you play.

Tackling

Always remember the advice given by Coach Wally Lemm of the St. Louis Cardinals on page 9, where he warns against the dangers of hesitating before making a tackle. He points out that slowing down before making any kind of body contact increases your chance of getting hurt, for you will receive almost all the shock of body impact. At the same time, a man running into you at full speed receives scarcely any shock.

A basic rule of tackling, then, is to *charge into your target at full speed.* Although it seems odd, the harder you hit your man the less you will feel the impact.

KEEP YOUR BODY LOW

Whenever possible (that is, whenever you get a good clean shot at your target) strike the ball carrier with your body leaning forward.

Never tackle a man while you are standing straight up, for in this position you are totally help-

36

less. You will be knocked flat on your back, and probably stunned. The sharper the angle at which you lean forward, the greater your striking power will be.

HIT YOUR TARGET WITH YOUR SHOULDER

Try to strike your man with the full force of one shoulder, rather than with your head. Use the shoulder that is nearer the approaching runner. If your target tries to dodge you at the last moment, you may hit him at an angle, and your head will be forced to one side. But you won't get hurt because your helmet will absorb the shock.

Don't, however, deliberately "spear" a runner with your helmet. This is dangerous, for it forces your neck to withstand his full weight. Your neck is one of the weakest parts of your body and should not be subjected to such deliberate punishment.

Don't get into the bad habit of "arm tackling," for even a weak runner can crash right through an outstretched arm. Reach out only if you are desperate, and have no chance of reaching the runner with your body.

Never dive at a runner approaching you. If he shifts his body even slightly, you will probably bounce off him. Leap at runners only when chasing them from behind or at a sharp angle, when you can't make a normal tackle.

Use the same short, digging steps in making a tackle that you would use in throwing a block. Short steps will give you more striking power, for your body momentum, or traveling force, is at a peak the instant you shove forward off one foot.

Don't glide through the air with long strides, for this prevents your legs from "digging" into the ground and launching your body forward with full force.

Short steps will also give you more control of your direction, allowing you to shift your body quickly to meet the changing path of a running back. If you take long steps, an approaching runner's change of direction may catch you in the middle of a stride—and he will speed right past you.

USE YOUR HANDS

Don't be afraid to use your hands once you have struck your opponent with your shoulder. It is perfectly legal to grab every part of a man's uniform except his helmet.

If you hit your man but fail to make a clean tackle, then try to grab his uniform. If you get a good grip on his jersey or trousers, he will be forced to drag you along as he runs. This will slow him down, and give other tacklers the chance to catch him. Even if you can only tug at his sleeve as he dashes by, it will slow him down a little bit.

TRY TO FOOL YOUR OPPONENT

Don't charge into your target in a straight line, like a bull making an attack. This will make it easy for him to judge your speed and to dodge you the instant before you reach him.

Try to confuse your opponent. Fake with your head and shoulders as he approaches you. Move your head, or dip one shoulder, to fake your tackle. Such a feint will force the runner to react by shifting his path away from what he thinks is your charge. Once he has been forced to do this, you will know his direction—and can charge into him at full speed.

In other words, try to *bluff* the runner into making the first move. If you are successful, you will have destroyed his ability to trick you, and he will be at your mercy.

In the NFL, an experienced runner and tackler approaching each other head on often engage in a "duel" of trickery. The winner will be the player who forces the other man to make the first move, and thereby give away his plan of attack.

Don't get into the habit of always faking in the same manner, or a running back will figure out your moves. Fake one time with your head, the next time with your shoulder, and never in the same precise manner or at the same distance from your target.

Remember that the key to successful tackling is to keep your opponent guessing—and to force him to make the first move.

ADJUST TO THE BALL CARRIER'S STYLE

A big, powerful fullback who relies on brute force rather than on trickery is an easy man to tackle, even if he terrifies you as he thunders toward you.

The secret of stopping such a "power runner" is simply to hit him in his weakest spot—below the knees. Striking him in this area will minimize the shock of impact, for most of his body weight is "high"—in his upper legs and torso. Hitting him below the knees will not only avoid the mass of his weight, but will also almost surely knock him down. Even the strongest man in football will be swept off his feet if his *balance,* rather than his power, is attacked.

So don't be afraid of hitting a big back at full speed. If your shoulder strikes him below the knees, he will hit the ground just like a smaller man.

Most halfbacks are lighter and faster than fullbacks, as are ends who are running with the ball after catching a pass. Instead of using leg power, such runners rely on shiftiness and on feinting with both their legs and bodies.

To stop this type of ball carrier you must adjust your style of tackling. Drive directly toward your man and fake a dive at his lower legs. This will force him to dance to one side. Then, as he makes his move, throw your shoulder at his waist. As you strike him, quickly wrap your arms around his body. Don't give him a chance to bounce off you. If he has dodged to one side just before you make body contact, you may be able to hold him with your arms. He won't have the same force as a power runner, since he will have sacrificed both straight-ahead speed and body momentum in trying to dodge to one side.

Don't ever try to tackle a tricky, shifty runner below the knees, for you may wind up with nothing but an armful of air. A skilled runner's legs are the easiest part of his body for him to shift from side to side. His upper body presents a far easier target to hit.

Not all running backs will be strictly power runners or tricky runners. Many will have some of the qualities of each. You will simply have to analyze every ball carrier you play against, and use good tackling technique and common sense to discover the best way to bring each one down.

Passing

The first step in throwing a forward pass is to get a good grip on the ball as soon as it is snapped back by the center.

It is just as important for a quarterback and his center to learn each other's habits as it is for a trapeze artist to know every move his partner makes. A quarterback who lacks control of the football as he backs away from the line cannot possibly have the necessary *ball control* to get off a good pass.

You must perfect the technique of taking the ball from the center until it becomes automatic for both of you. Practice by the hour, if necessary, until he can snap the ball right into your hands and you can get a good grip on it immediately.

To position your hands for receiving the ball, simply place your right hand firmly against the center's seat, and put your left hand about eight inches below the right. As he snaps the ball into your right hand, your left hand quickly comes up and locks on the bottom half of the ball.

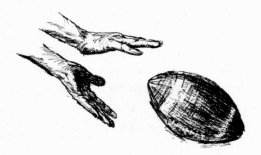

How you grip the ball depends on both the size of your hands and the length of your fingers. Most quarterbacks in the NFL hold the ball so that about two-thirds of its length is in front of the little finger.

Your fingers should be slightly spread, and placed across the laces of the ball. (Some passers prefer to rest their fingertips on the laces.)

Hold the ball firmly, but don't squeeze it with all your strength. Experiment until the ball feels

natural, or *balanced,* in your hand. There's no rule to follow because even boys of the same age have different sized hands and fingers.

One way to "test" your grip is to hold the ball above your head in a regular passing position. Then move your arm swiftly back and forth. If the ball tends to jump forward or backward out of your hand, you will have to adjust it until it feels comfortable.

A small boy learning how to pass may not be able to do more than balance the ball on top of

his hand—and pass by "rolling" the ball off his fingers. As his hands grow larger, he will be better able to squeeze the ball, gradually increasing both accuracy and distance.

DROPPING BACK TO PASS

The old-fashioned style of dropping back to pass (still used by some quarterbacks) is merely to trot backward in short, firm steps after taking the snap from the center.

But there is one great disadvantage to moving backward: The defense *knows* you are going to pass because they see the ball clearly with every step you take.

A much better way for a quarterback to move into passing position is simply to turn around (so that his back faces the line) and run. To see what the defensive line is doing, he looks back over his shoulder as he is moving. While "retreating," he can either hand the ball to a running back or quickly pivot into a passing position.

Since the defense will be looking at his back and cannot see the ball, they won't know what the quarterback plans to do *until he starts to do it*. This gives the offense a "head start," and greatly increases the chance of a play's resulting in a big gain.

Another advantage to "turning and running" is that you save a great deal of time getting into position. It is much quicker to run forward than it is to back up. And there is far less chance of tripping and falling while running forward, for you have much better control of your body.

FAKING

Every quarterback in the NFL has learned the need of faking a pass. For it is just as important

46

as being able to throw the ball right into the arms of a sprinting receiver.

Any quarterback who drops back into a passing position, then sets himself and flings the ball at once is foolish. He is wasting at least twenty-five percent of his natural ability—even if he is a great passer.

If instead, you fake a pass (by simply pumping your arm back and forth in a passing motion) you will throw the defensive team off stride. An on-rushing lineman cannot help reacting when he sees you are about to let the ball go. Nine out of ten times he will either slow up—deciding that he cannot reach you in time to prevent the pass—or leap high in the air to knock the ball down as it leaves your fingertips. In other words, faking makes the defense hesitate and thereby gives you *more time to pass.*

Even defensive halfbacks and safeties often cannot help reacting when they see a quarterback's arm start to come forward.

Every boy interested in becoming a quarterback should always fake once or twice before releasing the ball. (You must be careful, however, not to get into the habit of always faking exactly one or two times. If you do, the defense will quickly learn the pattern of your moves.)

When you get set to throw the ball, your body must be set, or ready.

No quarterback should pass with just his arm, unless he must throw the ball in a hurry to avoid onrushing defensive linemen. To get off a long pass, or even a strong short pass, the weight of your body must be behind your arm. You must plant your right foot on the ground (assuming you are right-handed), with most of your weight on the right side of your body.

Then, as you step forward to release the ball, your leg and body shoves forward, adding both power and accuracy to your pass.

THE PASSING MOTION

Most passers prefer to throw the ball with a three-quarter overhand action. But this is an individual matter. You must experiment to find the best method for your own arm. (A boy with very small hands may almost be forced to throw side-arm in order to keep his small hand under the ball.)

Nothing is more pleasing to the eye than a perfect spiral floating through the air. But every coach in the NFL prefers a passer who can throw the ball *accurately*—even if his spiral has a wobble.

Don't make the mistake of forcing your arm and hand forward in an unnatural manner, just to make the ball spiral perfectly. It is much wiser to develop a good throwing motion, accuracy, and distance.

To throw the ball, draw your arm back, lift your left arm for balance, and release the ball fairly high over your head, while stepping forward and shifting your weight to your left leg. (This will give you "body power" to back up your arm strength.)

As you can see in the drawing above, it is very important to release the ball high (rather than low, at shoulder level). A high release will give height to your pass, and will make it go farther than a low, flat pass. Also, a high release will lift the ball above the outstretched hands of onrushing linemen trying to block your pass.

"Following through" with your arm is the final step in throwing a good forward pass. Bring your hand down and over, so it ends up below the waist. If you follow through correctly, your body will have shifted so that your weight is forward on your left leg. Following through will help both the accuracy and distance of your passing.

Punting

Any boy can learn how to punt—but only if he is willing to *practice over and over again.*

Punting is a matter of balance and timing. A successful combination of the two can be achieved only by going through the proper motions literally hundreds of times.

It is far wiser for a boy to develop good habits and proper form than to emphasize kicking the ball for distance—even if he can only punt the ball 20 yards at first. In time, as he grows bigger and stronger, his kicks will naturally travel farther and farther. The ball will travel the greatest possible distance, however, only if he kicks it smoothly and with the correct foot and body movements.

Consistency is the single most important factor in punting. Many experienced punters in the NFL could probably close their eyes and get off a fairly good punt. They are able to do this not because they are great athletes or have a rare ability, but because they have trained their bodies to near perfection. They have practiced the correct motions thousands of times.

Good punting form can be illustrated with the following simple steps.

Punters stand from 10 to 15 yards behind the line of scrimmage. (Coaches position their punters according to such factors as the quickness with which the punter gets the ball away, the center's ability to feed him the ball chest high, and the blocking ability of the linemen.)

While waiting for the snap from center, place your legs comfortably apart. Lean slightly forward and bend your arms slightly while holding them outstretched about waist high. The palms of your hands should be about six inches apart and tilted slightly upward.

As soon as you catch the ball in both hands, shift it quickly so that the rear end of the ball is "stuck" in the palm of your right hand. Your left hand should hold the front of the ball to keep it steady. The lacing should be on top of the ball, and the nose should be pointed slightly downward and inward.

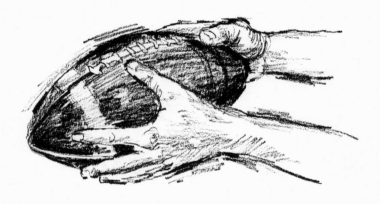

It is a good idea to get a center to practice with you. He can perfect his snapping back of the ball, while you are learning to shift it quickly into the proper position in your hands. The more you practice the faster you will be able to shift the ball, with less chance of fumbling.

Stand with your right foot approximately twelve inches in back of your left, with your weight on your left leg. Your arms should be partially extended and slightly bent.

As you take your first full step, stretch your arms out. *Keep your eye on the ball.* At the end of the step, allow your left arm to begin falling away from the ball.

As you take the second step with your left leg,

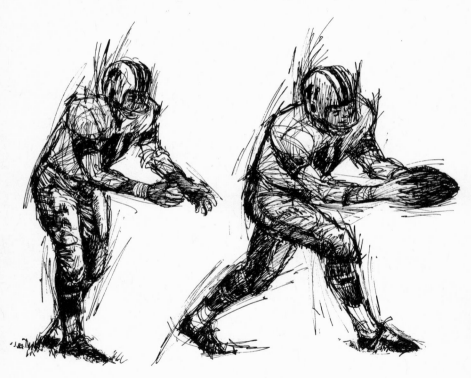

release the ball by gently removing your right hand. (Allow the ball to "hang" in the air; don't throw it toward the ground.) *With your eyes still on the ball,* land on your left leg, which should be slightly bent at the knee, and prepare to follow through with your kicking leg.

If you have released the ball correctly, it will fall toward the ground with its nose pointed slightly downward and inward as your right leg begins the kicking move.

Just before your foot meets the ball, you should be in a comfortable position, with your left foot on the ground but the weight of your body being transferred into the swing of your kicking leg. Your foot should meet the ball when it is still about two feet off the ground. This will vary, however, according to each kicker's build and height. Only by experimenting can you learn just how far off the ground the ball should be for *your* kick.

MEETING THE BALL

Your foot should be held firmly in a straight line. Do not bend it even slightly. You should meet the ball with the instep of your foot a little bit in back of the center of the ball. Since the ball has been falling with the nose pointed slightly to one side, it will "roll" off your foot at an angle, and a good spiral should result.

In order to get maximum distance and good accuracy you must follow through by lifting your leg high in the air. If you follow through with the proper force, the toes of your left foot should actually "take off" from the ground, lifting your body into the air.

Place Kicking

Position of the Ball   Use a kicking tee to support
the ball. Place the ball so that it stands almost
straight up, leaning slightly backward toward the
kicker. The laces should face forward, away from
you, so that your foot can't accidentally spin the ball
toward one side of the field by striking the laces.

Approaching the Ball
   Start far enough away to build up good momentum. (The yardage required for approaching the ball
differs with the individual, but nobody should need
more than 15 yards.)

Don't sprint at full speed, because this gives you "body bounce," which prevents your kicking the ball with a smooth, flowing motion.

Instead, run at a fairly fast trot so that your body is controlled and you approach the ball in a straight line, instead of swaying from side to side.

Stepping

Practice approaching the ball so that with your final step you land on your left leg—about 12 to 18 inches from the ball. As your left foot hits the ground, swing your kicking leg forward. At the very start of the kick, your upper leg should be no higher than your left leg, so that the power in your kicking leg is concentrated in a "snapping forward" motion, with the knee as a pivot.

The kicking foot must have the toes pointing up, with the foot held in a firm position.

The Moment of Impact

Your foot should strike the ball about two-fifths of the way up, or slightly below the center. *Keep your eyes on the ball until you have finished kicking it.*

If your foot strikes the ball too low, it will squirt high in the air and lack distance. If you kick it too high, the ball will take off in a straight line without any height. (Height is necessary, for it keeps

the ball in the air much longer than a low kick.
This gives your teammates more time to race downfield to tackle the back who catches the ball.)

When your foot meets the ball, you should be
leaning slightly forward for extra power.

Follow through with your leg, raising it high.
Your follow-through, which should actually cause
your body to leave the ground, adds both distance
and accuracy to your kick.

(The proper technique for holding the ball for the kicker is discussed on page 139, under, "Holding the Ball for Place Kicking." This section is concerned only with the kicking technique.)

In the NFL, the field goal is a potent scoring weapon. Again and again, booming 40- and 50-yard kicks split the goal posts. Often they win games in the final minutes of play. In school football, however, the field goal is used far less often. One reason is that the goal posts are set at the back of the end zone rather than on the goal line, making it necessary to kick the ball 10 yards farther than in the NFL. Few schoolboys have the leg power to kick a field goal from beyond the 20-yard line (a 30-yard kick).

But don't let that discourage you. Concentrate on developing *skill* and *accuracy*, so that when you are fully grown and have good leg power, you will be able to send the ball high and deep down the field.

The same fundamentals apply to kicking field goals as to kicking off. You need body balance and timing, which can be acquired *only by practice.* There must also be coördination among the center, the ball holder, and the kicker.

64

The Proper Footwork

While you stand waiting for the ball to be snapped from the center, lean slightly forward with your weight on your left foot. As the ball is

snapped, start your move forward—not with great speed, but at a good pace and with control of your body. Take your first step with your right foot. As the ball holder gets the ball and starts to place it on the ground, you should be starting your second step—with your left foot. (The foot should

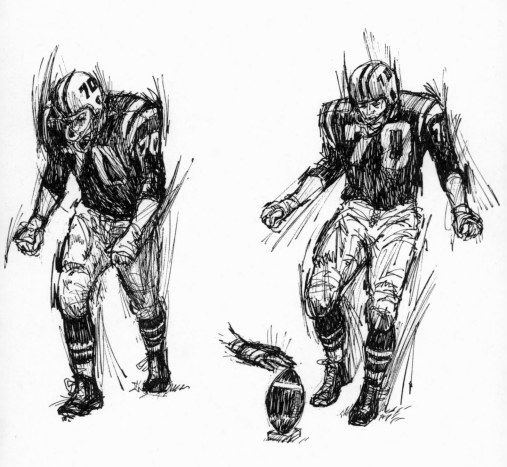

land from 12 to 18 inches from the ball.)

By this time the ball holder will have the ball firmly planted on the ground. Keeping your eye on the ball, swing into your kicking motion with your right leg. Hit the ball at the same spot you would in making a kick-off, and use the same fol-

low-through. Don't raise your eyes to follow the flight of the ball until it has left the ground.

Field goals are subject to the rush of defensive linemen, so there is a *time limit* to getting away your kick. You must make use of every fraction of a second.

There is no substitute for practicing with your center and ball holder—kicking field goals again and again. Practice using different angles and varying distances from the goal posts.

Making Adjustments

In addition to a kicker's natural fear of onrushing defensive linemen, two other factors often damage his accuracy: the wind and a kicking "rut." (He temporarily loses his feeling of rhythm and confidence, so that the ball keeps traveling too far to one side.)

If the wind is blowing from one side of the field to another, you must allow for it by estimating how far it will carry the ball. Naturally, you will have to adjust your kicking direction according to the stiffness of the wind. Always kick at least 20 practice field goals before a game. This will give you the "feel" of the wind, so you can kick with confidence during the game.

If you are in a rut (your kicks consistently travel too far to one side), you must compensate by aiming the ball slightly in the other direction. For example, if the ball has been traveling over the left side of the goal posts, you must aim your kick toward the right so that the ball will cross between the goal posts.

This is a procedure to follow only during a game, however, when you don't have time to discover the flaw in your kicking style. As soon as possible after the game, correct your kicking motion so that the ball consistently heads straight between the goal posts.

4

Playing Football—
Position by Position

You have learned how to block and how to tackle, as well as how to pass, punt, and place kick. You have learned what body balance means, how to protect yourself, how to approach your target, and how to use fakes. You will now learn how to apply all these basic techniques while playing your position on a football team.

Each position on a team will be fully analyzed from two points of view: First, the physical requirements which are necessary to play that position; secondly, the skills or techniques which you must develop to fill such a playing role.

Positions such as tackle and end, where a man

plays both offense and defense, will be treated as two separate positions.

In studying the basic physical requirements for the position you want to play, analyze yourself carefully. If you don't fulfill the requirements for playing such a role, don't stubbornly cling to the idea. Instead, adjust your thinking to the possibilities of playing a position for which your body and your talents are better suited.

Naturally, boys on most school teams will have to play both offense and defense, since school teams don't "platoon" their players (have separate offensive and defensive teams). A good offensive end, expert at catching passes, won't necessarily have the ideal build or strength to be as good at defensive end (where, ideally, a bigger man should play). But he should still learn how to play defensive end, for he might as well know the best way to do the job as long as he has to play the position. And *any* ability a boy develops will help him become a better athlete.

He should also develop his ability at both offensive and defensive end because it is not practical in high school football to become an expert player at just one position.

A team in the NFL may have as many as 10 or 12 tackles in training camp—all huge men weighing 250 pounds or more. The coach can eliminate them one by one, until he has kept perhaps five on the team. Then he can divide them according to their skill at playing either offensive or defensive football.

In schools, where the supply of raw manpower is usually very limited, a coach must use his best athletes as much as possible—often in positions where he wouldn't play them if he had a greater number of good players.

5
Linemen

Offensive End

The ideal end is tall and rangy, fast and shifty. Although ends are often pictured as skinny, a fairly big man who is light on his feet can also play the position well.

Besides natural speed, an end must have great ability to run tirelessly. Although some players train themselves for short bursts of speed, an end should train more like a mile runner. For in his role as a pass catcher, he must run down the field on almost every play. Even when he isn't going to catch a

75

pass, he must still run downfield as a "decoy." This forces a defensive back to follow him, leaving a certain area unguarded .

An end, unlike an interior linemen (center, guard, or tackle), doesn't have to be able to take great body punishment. His job is usually to *avoid* body contact in order to get free to catch a pass.

He must have the ability to *fake* defensive players out of position. Even if he is very fast and an excellent pass catcher, he can't do his job unless he can evade the man who is covering him. Defensive backs are often the fastest players on the field.

Finally, an end must have a good pair of hands so that he can hold onto the ball once he gets his fingers on it. If a player can't develop the ability to catch the ball while sprinting at full speed, or while suddenly changing direction, he will probably never become a good end.

Learning to catch passes isn't just a matter of running downfield and snatching perfect spirals out of the air. The next time you watch an NFL game, you will see some fantastic catches by ends who are way off balance, or who must suddenly stop in their tracks and leap high in the air. Often a receiver will even have to change his direction, or make a sudden dive and pluck the ball out of the air inches off the ground.

He doesn't develop this ability just by catching

perfectly thrown spirals. He spends hour after hour in practice, catching hundreds of passes.

Bucky Pope, speedy young end for the Los Angeles Rams, has a personal practice method that is valuable for developing good hands. Get a friend to throw passes at you. Ask him to deliberately make his aim bad so that you will have to jump to catch the ball.

Have him throw passes which are too wide, too low, or too high. Practice catching them while you are standing still and while you are running. Have him throw the ball from various distances and at different speeds. This is an excellent way to develop a good pair of hands.

FINE POINTS OF PLAY

The following diagram shows the possible routes ("pass patterns") an end can run. Notice the great choice of directions he has. This makes it important

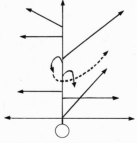

for the defensive team to slow him down as much as they can, or—if possible—to knock him off his feet before he gets started. The longer it takes an end to break into the clear, the less chance the quarterback has to hit him with a perfect pass. Don't forget that the quarterback, under pressure from rushing defensive linemen, doesn't have much time to throw the ball.

Gary Collins, a great offensive end for the Cleveland Browns, advises players to remember that an end can be blocked at the start of a play just like any other player. As soon as the ball is snapped from center, defensive players may legally dive at an end and knock him down. Or they can keep bumping him with their bodies as he moves downfield. Of course this can be done only until the moment the ball is thrown. If an end is touched after that, the referee calls "interference." This means that the pass is ruled complete in a case where the end would have caught the ball if he hadn't been touched.

Since an end is a target when the play starts, he must expect to be treated roughly as soon as the ball is snapped.

Develop good fakes as you start going downfield —to avoid getting hit.

Learn how to look in one direction and run in another. Fake going left with your head and shoulders, but jump to the right with your body. One trick is to rush straight at the defensive back covering you. Then, the instant before he tries to block you, dart to one side.

Another good trick is to fake throwing a block at the defensive end. This will make him think you are trying to block him because a running play will be heading in his direction. The linebacker, seeing you block the end, will also suspect a running play and will quickly move toward the line.

This leaves you free to suddenly stop blocking the end and dash past the surprised linebacker into the clear.

Of course you must learn to vary your fakes, so the man covering you won't catch on to your moves. There are no rules about faking. But by using your head, eyes, shoulders, and whole body you can feint a defending back off-balance, and sometimes right off his feet.

To make sure their ends get off to a fast start, many coaches in the NFL have them line up in a "split" position. Instead of standing beside the tackle, they move toward the sideline anywhere from 5 to 15 yards. This "isolates" the end at the start of a play. He can't be blocked by a defensive end or a linebacker, but is guaranteed a fast start down the field. His only battle will be with the defensive back assigned to cover him.

If you are learning to play end, you will soon discover that every defensive back you play against will use different techniques in trying to cover you. As a result, you must play your position in a flexible manner.

If your opponent is very strong, but not as fast as you are, fake a great deal and use your speed to break past him into the clear. Do everything in your power to avoid physical contact.

If your opponent is weak but very fast, rush right at him. Establish the fact that you are stronger than he is, and he'll be forced to run away from your initial charge. This will give you the chance to fake him toward one side of the field, so you can break quickly in the other direction.

Defensive End

PHYSICAL REQUIREMENTS

A defensive end should have good size, but he doesn't have to be as big as the defensive tackle who plays at his side. In the NFL, defensive tackles are usually the biggest men on the field.

In nine out of ten plays, a defensive end has one of two objectives. He must either tackle a running back or rush into the enemy backfield to get the quarterback before a pass is thrown. (Naturally, in order to do his job, he must fight off the man trying to block him.)

A defensive end must have *lateral mobility*. That is, he must have the speed to run to the sideline in time to prevent a fast runner from circling him on an "end sweep" and speeding down the field for a long gain. He must also have the toughness to fight off blockers while remaining on his feet.

Harland Svare, coach of the Los Angeles Rams, talks about his great defensive end, Dave Jones.

Dave has everything it takes to be a great defensive end. He moves his 261 pounds like a cat. He's great at taking punishment, never gets discouraged, and is such a keen student of the game that he is rarely fooled on a play.

He's perfect proof of my theory that a good defensive end should be part tiger and part bear. For he knows how to fight his way past blockers, rush to the sidelines to cut off enemy runners, and has such wonderful fakes that the offensive tackle assigned to block him is always guessing.

A defensive end must develop the ability to make short, fast charges again and again without getting tired. He rarely has to sprint 30 or 40 yards like an offensive end. *But he must be able to get off to a quick start, for two reasons.*

First, he must be quick enough to "cut off" a running back, even when he can't make a tackle. In other words, he must be able to get in the path of the runner, forcing him to leap to one side. This not only slows the back down but also increases the chance of another defensive player's making a tackle.

Secondly, a fast start gives him good body momentum, which he needs to charge past the tackle trying to block him.

A defensive end should develop as much strength as possible in his hand and arm muscles, since defensive players are allowed to grab offensive players with their hands.

FINE POINTS OF PLAY

A defensive end's job is completely different from that of an offensive end. The offensive end depends upon speed and trickery to get into the clear; sometimes he can avoid all body contact. The defensive end must often depend upon strength and aggressiveness to fight, scramble, or power his way past a blocker trying to stop him.

There are three basic routes into the enemy backfield: to the outside, inside, or right "through" the man trying to block you. In the NFL, defensive ends rarely try using brute force to knock over offensive tackles. A tackle with good body balance will simply let you bounce off him, reset his body, and be ready for your next charge. Or he may quickly step to one side and let you come crashing through, so you will be hit from the side—and knocked flat—by a "trap block" by another lineman.

In deciding how to attack the man blocking you, take advantage of the way he plays you. See if he is subject to being drawn off balance by a certain type of fake—either with your head, shoulders, eyes, or a false start with your whole body.

Learn if he has a particular weakness. For instance, some offensive linemen are deadly when it comes to stopping you from rushing around them (going to their outside). But they aren't nearly as skilled at keeping you from cutting to their inside.

Doug Atkins, the 255-pound defensive end of the Chicago Bears, thinks of himself as a wrestler and the opposing offensive tackle as a boxer. He feels that he has the great advantage of being able to use his hands to grab any part of the opponent's body or uniform except the helmet bars across his face.

The offensive lineman can only shove you, butt you with his body, or "chop" at your arms with his own to keep you from getting a grip on him. You must learn to fight off your opponent's arm blows in order to grab him.

Learn to move your hands quickly, making fake lunges until you find an opening. Then grab him and hang on with all your strength. This is the first part of the battle between any defensive lineman and the blocker trying to stop him.

Some tackles are so intent on keeping you from grabbing them that they forget all about their body balance while shoving your hands away. If your opponent makes this mistake, and forgets to lean forward, surprise him by suddenly ramming your body into his with all your force. He will tumble over backward.

If, on the other hand, a tackle gets into the habit of playing you only with his body, he will be hard to knock down, for his legs will be firmly "planted." But since he will be concentrating on his balance and forgetting your arms, you can grab him with your hands.

Whenever you get a good grip on your opponent, shove or twist him in the direction you catch him leaning: forward, backward, or to one side. But don't keep your own body rigid as you try to move him out of the way, because your arms alone just don't have the strength to move another player's body.

Instead, move quickly and spin your own body around his—just as if you were pivoting while holding onto a pole planted in the ground. In other words, use your opponent as a "springboard," and propel yourself away from the weight of his body.

Sensing the "flow" of a play (the direction it will take) is an ability which is developed only with years of play. In your duel with a tackle, allow for the fact that he may be clever. He may jump to your left side just to make you think the play is going to be run to your left, even though he knows it will be run to the right. If you respond to his trick and leap to your left to stop the play, you may find the ball carrier racing through the spot you just vacated.

But don't try to anticipate a play just by observing the motions of the man playing against you.

Instead of assuming that you have guessed your opponent's intention, and making a fast move based on this guess, stay put and wait until you are *certain* of what is happening. If you don't try to guess the opponent's plays, you won't be fooled.

Of course there is no substitute for experience. The longer you play, the better your ability will be to "feel" what type of play the offense is planning to use—and the stronger your chances will be of stopping it.

Offensive Tackle

PHYSICAL REQUIREMENTS

An offensive tackle doesn't need great speed. But since good speed is an asset in any position, don't rule yourself out of playing the position if you are lucky enough to be fast as well as big.

An offensive tackle must be an outstanding blocker, for often his assignment is to block a hard-charging defensive end. For this job he needs not only strength and size but also a powerful pair of legs to keep "digging" into the ground to sustain his blocks.

Although a tackle doesn't need running speed, he should have quick hand, arm, and body movements. He should also be able to shift his weight from side to side in order to stand off the thrusts of his opponent.

FINE POINTS OF PLAY

Bob Vogel, outstanding young tackle of the Baltimore Colts, weighs only 235 pounds, as compared with the 260 pounds of many of the defensive ends whom he must block. But Bob does his job so consistently that he is recognized as one of the bright young stars of the NFL. In the following paragraphs, Bob discusses the basic techniques of playing his position:

Many boys think an offensive tackle is a stone wall. But instead of planting himself at the line of scrimmage like a bull, a really skilled tackle plays a "flowing" position. He is light on his feet and ready to move quickly. He doesn't fight a battle of muscle, but shifts his body quickly and skillfully in order to stop the thrusts of his opponent.

As long as you keep balanced, and lean forward with your shoulder muscles rigid and your arms high in front of you, no defensive player can crash right through you. Even if he is stronger than you and can charge with more force, you can engage him in a "bumping duel." You may gradually have to give up ground, but in so doing you will be winning the battle. For in keeping him occupied with you, you are stopping him from tackling a runner or reaching your quarterback.

Don't look into your opponent's eyes. Keep looking at his arms.

You can be faked right out of your shoes by a man's eyes, for he can simply look in one direction and go in another. The defensive player's arms are often his best weapons, for he is allowed to grab you, shove you forward or backward, or twist your body to the side. A good defensive lineman can use your body like a springboard, "launching" himself away from you with a stiff shove of his arms.

Another important point to remember is that *time is on your side.* The longer an offensive lineman can prevent his opponent from carrying out his job, the greater are his team's chances to run a successful play. The pressure is on the defensive lineman to reach a runner or passer. As each sec-

87

ond ticks by, the chances of his succeeding grow
fewer and fewer.

If you keep your opponent busy fighting you,
you are winning your personal battle with him,
even if you are getting knocked all over the field.

Take a look at the following diagram, and you
will see how a tackle is forced to keep "bumping"
a defensive end again and again.

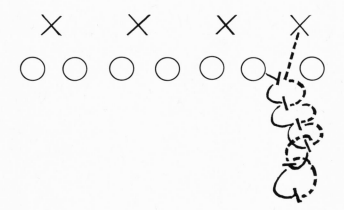

Notice that the tackle must shift quickly to meet
the repeated thrusts of the end, and must be willing
to gradually sacrifice ground while making sure he
stays between his opponent and the football. While
keeping his body firm, the tackle lets himself "flow"
with the direction of the end's charge.

Although a tackle's job is usually to block out a
single opponent, he should remain alert once that

job is done. He should not make the mistake of relaxing and considering the play finished. For he may be able to throw another block at another charging defensive player.

Always look for a close target as long as you are still on your feet. Until the referee's whistle officially ends the play, you are permitted to throw a block at every man wearing the enemy uniform. In the NFL, fast tackles often throw key blocks for running backs 30 or 40 yards downfield.

But *don't* be foolish and decide to make a spectacular play by blocking two men at once from your position on the line. You will be overreaching yourself, and will probably end up missing both your assigned opponent and the second target.

Only try to block a second opponent after you have successfully blocked your primary target out of the play.

Jim Ray Smith, the great offensive tackle of the Dallas Cowboys, has just about the same speed, strength, and skill as most of the other tackles in the NFL. But he has developed one special talent that has helped him to stay for nine years in a league as tough as the NFL: *his ability to analyze his opponents.* He makes it a point to concentrate on every little detail of their playing methods in order to discover their weak spots and take advantage of them.

Jim has learned that no two defensive ends play alike. Some have great ability to charge to your left, others to your right, and some move so quickly they can catch you napping and bowl you over backward.

Some have tremendously strong legs and can drive into you with the power of a horse. Some don't have much leg drive, but rely on balance and grabbing you with their hands. Others step quickly from side to side, relying on trickiness to dance past you.

Every opponent Jim faces has one favorite method of attack. By preventing him from using this technique, Jim cuts down the number of times that players manage to charge past him.

For example, if a defensive end is unusually skilled in jumping to your left and grabbing you, destroy his advantage by moving your starting position on the line a few inches to the left. This will force him to come at you more from the right side, where he has only ordinary ability. By depriving him of his strongest move, you will make him play *your* game.

Jim Smith is convinced that even offensive tackles on high-school teams can find weaknesses in their opponents during the course of a single game. Most young defensive linemen don't vary their moves enough. They charge in only one direction, or always grab their opponent's uniform with the same hand.

So follow Jim's technique. Concentrate on preventing your opponent's strongest method of attack, and you will reduce his ability as a player.

Defensive Tackle

PHYSICAL REQUIREMENTS

Defensive tackles are usually the biggest men on a football team. This is because they have two key jobs: to crash into the enemy backfield in order to tackle the quarterback before he can throw a pass, and to stop the offensive team's heaviest, strongest runner—usually the fullback, who runs "power plays" through the line. (Defensive ends usually must stop lighter, less powerful halfbacks, who run "wide plays" toward the outside of the line.)

Although skill and proper playing techniques are always important, a defensive tackle must have certain physical characteristics or all the strategy in the world won't help him. He must have great size, toughness, and powerful legs, for he is sure to be hit again and again by the other team's best blockers. Often these are the offensive guards, who have a running start because they "pull out" of the line the instant the ball is snapped from center. As a result, they gather great momentum, so the man they hit must have bulk and power to keep from being knocked down or driven backward.

Even if a defensive tackle "beats" an enemy lineman and charges into the offensive backfield, he will often face a second challenge—the blocking of the fullback. This usually happens on passing plays, in which the fullback helps to protect the quarterback. Since there are often several men charging him, a defensive tackle must be able to take great punishment.

A defensive tackle does not need great speed. Unlike a defensive end, who must play carefully and wait to see how a play is developing, the tackle can take a chance by rushing with all his strength into the offensive line whenever he believes that he has guessed the coming play. Even if he guesses wrong, he won't be far out of position.

He can play a more wide-open game than the defensive end because the area he must cover is much smaller. The end not only must cover his own part of the defensive line, but must be ready and able to dash all the way to the sideline to stop a wide run. If he makes a bad guess about a play, he may find himself as much as 10 or 15 yards away from the ball carrier. The defensive tackle, on the other hand, has a much smaller area to cover, and can't be caught so far out of position.

This is particularly true in school and sandlot football, where the tackle plays between the defensive end and defensive guard and must cover only the narrow strip of ground between the two players. In the NFL there are no defensive guards, for the defensive team lines up differently. Two defensive ends line up outside two defensive tackles, backed up by three linebackers.

FINE POINTS OF PLAY

Even an experienced tackle who is good at faking and squirming past his opponents should occasionally try to crash through the enemy line by using plain brute force.

If he succeeds in spilling a runner for a loss or flattening the quarterback before he can pass, he will have won a great psychological advantage (besides stopping the play for a loss). He will be considered a strong threat for the rest of the game. As a result, the offense may be "scared" into avoiding him by unconsciously hurrying their plays. This destroys their timing and often leads to fumbles.

Not only must a defensive tackle be able to "blast" past a blocker but he also must be able to squirm, or fake, his way past an opponent. He should remember that as long as a blocker keeps him occupied, he can't do his job—even though he is pushing that blocker steadily backward.

93

As a defensive lineman, you have to remember that you can be taken out of a play without being budged an inch. Nothing is more frustrating to a huge tackle than a "bumping" duel with a smaller blocker, especially if a back carrying the ball dashes past just inches out of his reach.

To avoid this, a defensive tackle must be able to play an extremely aggressive game. He must learn to make a savage charge. Also, he must use good body motions and every ounce of strength in his arms and hands to hurl an opponent away from him, thus freeing himself to make a tackle.

On school teams, the defensive tackles will probably be the heaviest players. They may outweigh their teammates to such an extent that they can forget about being clever and making fakes and can simply crash through the offensive line using raw power.

But they won't get away with such an obvious attack for a whole game. A smart coach will have two blockers double-team such a powerful defender, or will have a guard "trap-block" him from the side.

Sometimes in an NFL game you will see a big tackle smash through the line and smear the ball carrier or passer for a big loss. But more often than not he succeeds with this move only because his teammates have coöperated with him in an all-out rush. This surprise move, called a "red dog," occurs when all the defensive linemen and even one or more linebackers put on a tremendous rush. (Both the defensive tackle and end may strike at the same spot in the offensive line, making it easy for the tackle to come bursting through.)

Jack Christiansen, coach of the San Francisco Forty-Niners, offers some valuable playing tips to boys learning how to play defensive tackle.

You must study your opponents carefully, for nearly all offensive linemen have at least one weakness. Use the opening minutes of a game to "feel out" your opponent. Experiment by charging first to his right, and then to his left. Surprise him by rushing into him like a bull. Try different fakes, and learn how easy or how hard it is to grab him with your hands.

Study how he uses his body, arms, hands, and legs. Discover if his reactions follow a *pattern*. In other words, see if he always reacts the same way to the same move on your part. For example, every time you try to grab his jersey with your left hand, he may shove at your wrist with his right arm. If you can predict his moves, then you will have him where you want him.

Once you discover an opponent's weakness— the easiest way to get by him—don't "waste" this knowledge by using it again and again. He will realize that you have discovered his weakness and use this discovery to stop you.

Instead, *save your best move for plays which count the most*—the critical moments when the result of a single play will determine if your team wins or loses the game.

Offensive Guard

PHYSICAL REQUIREMENTS

An offensive guard must have "a little bit of everything"; he should be fast, fairly big (not necessarily as big as a tackle), very tough, and an *excellent* blocker. And he must be able to take consistent punishment.

Although the offensive tackle can often get away with fighting a "delaying action" (by giving ground as he keeps fighting off an attacking defensive end), guards are truly offensive players. They are required to throw blocks all over the field.

FINE POINTS OF PLAY

A guard must be able to throw several types of blocks. First, there is the ordinary straight-ahead block in which he duels head-to-head with a single opponent lined up across from him. Secondly, he must be able to throw a "trap" block (described in detail in the blocking section).

In throwing blocks at a man playing opposite him on the line, the guard uses the same basic techniques as a tackle.

But to lead a ball carrier as a running blocker, a guard must develop a special talent called "pulling out" of the line. (This is a specialized skill used only by guards.)

"Pulling out" means simply stepping back and away from the line and, in one smoothly coördinated move, running parallel to and behind the line, as the diagram below illustrates.

Guards in the NFL have perfected this skill so that they start their movement the instant the ball is snapped from center. Less than a second later they are running toward the sidelines.

The art of "pulling out" is explained in the following series of diagrams, which show a guard "pulling out" to the right. The same technique is used for a guard moving to the left, except that he uses the opposite parts of his body.

Notice that the guard starts the play lined up in the lineman's classic starting position, with his weight properly divided between his arm and legs. But his left foot must be about 12 inches ahead of his right so that he can use the right foot as a pivot.

As soon as the ball is snapped from the center, he

begins his move—pulling his body back from the line and quickly moving his arms, legs, and body at the same time.

As he pivots, or twists his body to the right, he increases the speed of this move by "snapping" both arms with great force. As he brings his right arm back, he shoves his left arm forward.

At the same time, he swings the weight of his

body around to the right by pivoting smoothly on his right foot. Then he quickly crosses his left leg over in front of his right leg and *continues* moving his left foot to take his first step as he drives into a full running motion. By "shoving off" hard on his right foot, he will pick up speed quickly. Pumping his arms as he runs will also help him gain speed.

Guards in the NFL who have perfected this move can pull out of a line and be running at good speed in an amazingly short time. But since pulling out automatically results in a running start, a guard must also learn how to throw a good block while running. This, too, is a special skill which requires practice. It is entirely different from the kind of block in which you "bump" a man lined up opposite you.

Pulling out allows a guard to cut suddenly, or turn into any place on the defensive line and act as a blocker ahead of the ball carrier.

Under some methods of play, he is supposed to block the first opponent who gets in his way. The blockers behind him then pick out other defensive targets. Under another system, he is assigned a specific man to block.

But no matter what system of play a coach uses, the guard must know how to throw running blocks with great body control. (Remember the warning in the section on blocking, which explained the dangers of hurling yourself off balance at an opponent. If you miss, you will land on your nose and be completely useless to your team.)

Ray Lemek, the superb offensive guard of the Pittsburgh Steelers, knows that, to throw a block while running, a guard must have excellent body control. This requires him to resist the temptation to run at full speed. For if he runs too fast, he won't be able to make sudden moves to either side without abruptly "jamming on the brakes." And stopping will take away all his momentum, so that he might as well be throwing the block while standing still.

To throw a running block, Ray travels at a *good* speed, but not at *full* speed, until he approaches his target, or is ready to make a sudden cut into the line. Then, he suddenly speeds up and attacks his man with full force. He hits him at just the right angle, because he has control of his direction.

Ray thinks the principle involved is the same as that of a fighter throwing a punch. If he aims a long punch at his opponent but, just after he swings, realizes he is off target, his reflexes will make him try to change the direction of the punch. As a result, it won't land with full force. Instead, it will arrive at an odd angle. This is similar to a guard running full speed at a moving opponent, and having to slow down suddenly and adjust his direction.

But if a fighter waits carefully until the other boxer makes a mistake and becomes a perfect target, he can let go with a punch that travels no more than 12 inches—yet knocks down his opponent. Ray feels this is similar to a guard "cruising" rather than sprinting toward his opponent, waiting to throw all his force into a block he knows he can't miss.

A guard must also have the ability to throw running blocks with varying degrees of force, depending on the situation and the play his team has called.

On some plays, the guard will be doing his job if he only knocks an opponent slightly off balance. This is true in a "quick-opening" play, in which the runner takes the ball at once and races through a small, quickly opened hole in the line.

In this situation an intelligent guard will use just enough force to knock his man out of position, for the runner needs only a second to zip through the hole. The guard, still on his feet, can then go charging into another man, or race downfield in the hope that he can be of help. A guard without such good judgment might flatten his opponent. But in the process *he* would fall down, too, thereby spoiling any chance of his hitting another target.

At other times a play may be called that doesn't send the back through the line so quickly. In such a play—a "delayed handoff," for instance, or a trick play in which several backs handle the ball—the guard *must* throw a hard block at an opponent.

Of course on many plays the defense will make sudden shifts, and the guard will have to make lightning-fast decisions about whom to block, how to block, or how fast to throw a block. The ability to make such decisions comes only with great experience.

Like any other player, a guard must make a study of his opponents' habits. But instead of analyzing only the man who plays across the line from him, he must learn about *every player he may have to block*—even the linebackers and defensive halfbacks.

Playing guard is a big job, and one that requires a tremendous amount of practice. It is not a "glamorous" position, but every coach in the NFL knows he can't develop a good running attack without a pair of outstanding guards.

Defensive Guard

There are no defensive guards in the NFL. Instead, two ends and two tackles make up a four-man front line of defense, backed up by three linebackers.

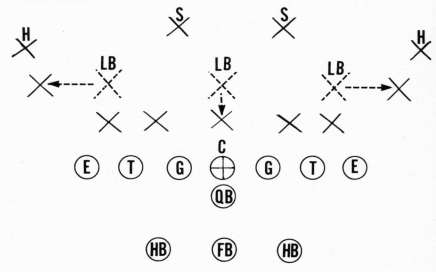

But many school and college teams do use guards on the defensive line.

PHYSICAL REQUIREMENTS

In his position in the center of the line, a defensive guard has a job much like that of a defensive tackle. A defensive guard can be a little smaller than the tackle, however, since he won't have to fight off as many blockers running ahead of a ball carrier. It's much harder for an offensive team to send blockers ahead of a ball carrier into the center of the line, where the defensive guard plays. Instead, plays run through that area are usually "quick openers." Quick blocks are thrown on the line, only a small hole is opened, and the ball carrier dashes through the line.

A defensive guard should be big, strong, and hard to budge. It will be greatly to his advantage if he has strong, thick legs. He must be an excellent, fast tackler, for often he must react very quickly in trying to grab running backs as they slice through the center of the line. He must develop excellent close-range agility—the ability to move his body quickly and repeatedly within a small area, in order to plug up holes opened up by offensive blockers for running backs.

A defensive guard does not need great speed. But like any defensive lineman he must have fast body reactions. And he must be able to take punishment without slowing down or losing his effectiveness.

A defensive guard must develop a good, tricky charge into the offensive line. Study the basic T formation lineup on page xi, and you will see why.

Notice that the defensive guard can be hit by the offensive guard and the center at the same time. (This is called "double-teaming.") If a defensive guard senses a passing play and fights his way through the line to get the quarterback, he may find the fullback waiting for him. The fullback is often used as an extra blocker on passing plays.

Perhaps a defensive guard's toughest job is on running plays, where he must hold his ground without making a strong charge. He must be able to fight off blockers and at the same time hold his position so that he can make tackles.

Plugging up his part of the line is a tough job. To develop this ability, a guard must learn to avoid becoming an easy target. He can do this by using his body in short, powerful thrusts against his opponent. He must never stand still, or allow himself to be hit while at a temporary halt as he shifts his body weight. The man striking him at such a moment will have enough body momentum to drive the guard out of his defensive position.

105

Center

Center is only an offensive position, for there is no such position as "center" on the defensive team.

On school and college teams, the offensive center usually plays linebacker on defense. In the NFL, the center plays only on offense, since professional teams have separate offensive and defensive units.

PHYSICAL REQUIREMENTS

Center is the one position on a team where a really slow runner won't be handicapped by lack of speed. For the center is the most stationary of all the offensive linemen. On running plays, he must throw a "holding block" at an opponent (that is, keep a defensive player from crashing past him). On passing plays, he is literally the center, or "anchor," of the offensive line. He must be as tough as granite, ready to block anyone who charges him (usually either a defensive lineman or a linebacker pulling a surprise move by trying to shoot through the line before a play gets really started).

Naturally a center must be able to snap the ball to the quarterback, as well as to spiral the ball to a back standing some seven or eight yards behind the line, or to a punter standing as far as fifteen yards deep. He must also be able to snap the ball at knee height to the man who holds the ball for the place kicker on field goal attempts.

In snapping the ball, a center must develop a smooth, flowing motion—whether he is only handing the ball to the quarterback or spiraling it 15 yards deep. There are no rules for gripping the ball because every center's hands are a different size. The ideal method of centering the ball is to use just one hand, as in the following drawing.

Note that the fingers are spread wide, with the fingertips placed across the laces for a better grip. About two-thirds of the ball should be behind your hand, toward the quarterback.

Boys who can't grip the ball with one hand should use two hands, as in the following drawing.

A center must have complete control of the football while it is in his possession. Poor control will mean a lack of both sureness and hand speed. Since the defense can hit a center the instant he moves his body, a center with slow reflexes can be jolted into fumbling the ball.

To get the ball to your quarterback, snap it up quickly and firmly (but don't *rush* the move) against the inside of his right hand. He will be pressing the upper part of his right hand against the seat of your pants. This is a simple motion, but to do it smoothly and with confidence you must practice with your quarterback until both of you are absolutely sure of your timing and the feel of each other's moves.

Avoid looking down. Always keep your head raised high so you can watch the defensive players in front of you.

Snapping the ball to a punter or place kicker requires a great deal of practice. Grip the ball in your hand (or hands) firmly but comfortably, and practice "snapping" it by using both your wrist and arm. Boys with small hands will have to rely more on arm movement and will have to "push" the ball. A man with a big hand can "flip" the ball with just his wrist and forearm.

Practice rolling the ball off your fingertips as your arm snaps back, and you will develop accuracy. (Imagine that you are a quarterback, passing the ball upside down.) With practice, you can develop a good spiral. This is important, for it is far easier for a back to catch a spiral than a ball tumbling wildly through the air.

Mick Tingelhoff, the outstanding young center of the Minnesota Vikings, knows a good method of practice which will help you perfect both your spiral and your aim: Mark several chalk spots on the wall of your house or garage. Make one spot at the height a back or punter would get the ball, and another at knee height, where a man holding the ball for a place kicker would be kneeling.

Then practice centering the ball again and again from different distances. Gradually, you will be able to hit your target consistently. Eventually, you won't have to peer back between your legs as you release the ball.

Good centers in the NFL can send the ball spinning right into the hands of a back while looking straight ahead—without even seeming to take aim. But they have developed this ability only after hours of practice. Of course, guiding the football through the air is only part of a center's job. He must also serve on the offensive line as a blocker.

Joe Kuharich, coach of the Philadelphia Eagles, talks about the importance of a center's having a good stance in order to block effectively.

The center does not take his position on the line like other offensive linemen, resting part of his weight on one hand placed on the ground. Instead, he must use that hand to grip the football. As a result, he must depend more on balancing his body with his legs.

This means he has good upright balance, but no "forward balance," and makes an easy target either to grab and pull forward on his nose or to charge into and knock flat on his back. There is nothing the center can do to avoid having to take such a stance, for his weight *must* be on his legs so his arm can move freely and easily in centering the ball.

But he can develop *speed* to make up for being an easy target at the moment he centers the ball. If he centers the ball very quickly, without warning the opposition of the split second he will move, then he can jump into a ready position. That is, he can shift his balance and quickly throw his arms up in front of his face in the standard blocking stance.

In other words, the center must use his arm and body speed to get into a protective position immediately after he centers the ball.

The center who *telegraphs* his moves (lets the opposition know the exact instant he plans to start the play by centering the ball) will be at a great disadvantage. Defensive linemen will be on top of him instantly and he will be helpless to resist their charge.

To avoid this, *the center must be careful not to "tip off" the opposition to the exact second he snaps the ball.*

To prevent defensive players from being able to "read" your move, get your coach and teammates to watch you carefully during both games and practice sessions.

Have them study every move you make, to see if

you are "giving away" the precise second when you will snap the ball. There are any number of ways in which you can unwittingly tip off the opposition. You may hold the ball loosely until you actually get ready to center it, and then squeeze it hard. This may flatten out your fingers, and a smart opponent will notice the change. Or you may suddenly stiffen your body just before you snap the ball, or lift your head up an inch.

Any such habit may be spotted by a rival, and can mean you will have a very rough afternoon of play. Practice constantly to snap the ball the same way every time. And make every movement with the same precise motions of your hand, fingers, body, head, and eyes.

Besides asking others to study your technique, practice at home in front of a mirror. Investing a few hours in perfecting your centering technique will pay off. Knowing that the opposition can't "read" your moves will give you more confidence and will make you a better player.

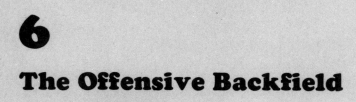

6
The Offensive Backfield

Quarterback

Anyone who has ever watched a football game knows that a quarterback must be able to pass. But a boy with exceptional passing ability will not automatically become a good quarterback. There is far more to playing the position than throwing a football.

A quarterback should be a natural athlete with fast reflexes, *both physical and mental.*

He should have deft hands—flexible, strong, and sure in their movements. He should operate his

115

whole body easily, smoothly, and fluidly. Physical rhythm is a vital ingredient of playing the position because so many other players must depend on his movements, such as backs to whom he hands off the ball.

He must be a quick thinker, able to make fast decisions while the ball is actually in play.

A quarterback must be willing to assume the responsibility of acting as the team's leader on the field, whether or not he calls the plays. Many quarterbacks *are* allowed to call the team's plays, except in situations where a coach spots a weakness on the defensive team, and sends in a play he is sure will work. But even when the coach calls every play, the quarterback is still the key player in making the ball move. He must work quickly, smoothly, and confidently both in handling the ball and in coördinating the efforts of his teammates. If they do not have great confidence in him, they will be playing at a great disadvantage.

A quarterback does not have to be a fast runner. But he must have *excellent body control.* Beyond the factors of timing and rhythm, he must be able to move quickly from side to side in order to dodge attacking defenders when he is trying to pass.

In passing, the quarterback must have more than the ability to throw the ball accurately and for distance. The longer he can wait to get rid of the ball, the more time he has to spot a receiver in the open field. If he relies on a "pushing" motion with his arm, rather than a quick arm movement and snap of the wrist, he will lack the ability to throw a pass while a defensive lineman is clinging to one of his legs. In other words, passing is not just a matter of throwing. It is releasing the ball *strongly and quickly*. And the quarterback must also be able to remain calm under pressure, for often he must fire the ball at the *last possible second* before being tackled. He must also be fearless, for a quarterback who cringes at the sight of an onrushing defensive lineman can't throw a good pass.

Tom Landry, coach of the Dallas Cowboys, has explained how hard it is to find good quarterbacks in the NFL, and offers some excellent advice to boys who are trying to learn this difficult position.

It's very hard to find "natural" quarterbacks. By this I mean a young player who has all the proper instincts for playing the position, as well as a good passing arm, good reflexes, and the ability to make decisions under great pressure.

I'm not saying that the quarterback is the most valuable player on a team. But it's a lot easier to "discover" a great tackle, or fullback, or even defensive safety. Such players can be measured quickly in terms of fundamentals: size, speed,

117

strength, blocking and tackling ability, toughness, and durability. These are qualities which can be seen at once.

But the same yardstick cannot be applied to a young quarterback, because his job is so complex that it would be unfair to judge him before he has had *years* to learn to put all his abilities together. His job requires not only basic skills, but *an instinct which can be developed only by experience.*

In the NFL it is very rare to see a college quarterback step right into a starting position. College stars who have received great publicity often sit on the bench during their first one or two seasons in the NFL. They are sent into action only in situations where the coach feels the pressure is off, and where a few mistakes can't really do any damage.

If it takes so long to become a good quarterback in the NFL, you can see why it's often impossible to judge a young boy's ability at the position.

I don't mean to discourage any boy from becoming a quarterback, if he is a good passer for his age and has been encouraged by his coach to continue playing the position. But remember that quarterback is a glamorous playing role and that in every school many athletes have their hearts set on that position.

By the time you get to college, there will be even tougher competition. There may be *several* outstanding quarterbacks who were stars in high

118

school. Even if you excelled in your own school, it may turn out that one of these boys is just a shade better than you.

That's why I think every boy should *become a complete football player*—not just a quarterback. It is the only way to take out "insurance" against having to sit on the bench and watch your teammates in action. Develop *all* the skills of the game, and learn how to play all the positions for which your abilities and body are suited.

Don't give up the idea of becoming a quarterback. Give it every effort, and perfect all the skills the position demands. But be ready to accept another role on the team.

Remember that playing any position is better than not playing at all.

FINE POINTS OF PLAY

In the chapter on passing, you learned many of the finer points in playing quarterback. You began with taking the ball from center and ended with following through properly with your arm.

But such lessons were concerned with passing rather than with actually playing the position. There are other important skills that a quarterback must develop.

119

Exchanging the Ball (*Handing the ball off*)

Consistency is the most important factor in handing the ball off to running backs. It must be handed to them the same way every time—thrust at them at the same speed, at the same height, and with your arms extended in exactly the same position. If you hand the ball to a running back a different way on every play, you not only make him slow up and lose both speed and confidence but you can also cause a fumble. If he is still holding the ball loosely as he hits the line, it is perfectly legal for defensive players to swat it out of his arms.

Study the following drawings to learn the art of handing the ball off properly.

Notice that you must plant your feet comfortably apart, so you can "swing" your body back and forth while your arms and legs are locked in place. In holding the ball, your elbows are held firmly at your hips. This position looks cramped, but it is actually not at all uncomfortable.

You should bend over slightly, to keep your body from becoming rigid, and hold the ball directly out in front of your belt buckle.

Don't push the ball hard into the stomach of a back running by. Instead, hold the ball motionless for an instant so the back can pick it out of the air.

There are two reasons for not extending your arms too far. First, you will lack ball control. It's

harder to hold the ball the same exact distance from your body repeatedly if your arms are partially outstretched. If one of your backs accidentally runs into you, you are likely to fumble. But if you keep your elbows against your hips, the ball will automatically extend no farther than the length of your forearms and hands. Secondly, if you hold the ball out too far from your body, every member of the opposition can see it very clearly.

Always *fake* at least one handoff, either before or after actually getting rid of the ball.

Never simply hand the ball off and then suddenly stop moving. In the first place, defensive players may crash into you while you are standing still. Also, in stopping your motion you make it clear that you have gotten rid of the ball. Then the entire defense will concentrate on the runner, instead of wondering who has the ball.

One good method of faking after you have made a handoff is to run back as if you are going to pass. (Look back over your shoulder to make sure you are not about to be hit by a defensive player.) This move forces at least part of the defense to keep concentrating on you. They can't be *sure* you don't have the ball unless they get a good look at you. Even though they will probably try to tackle the running back who is actually carrying the ball, they won't be able to concentrate only on him as long as there is any chance that you are holding the ball.

Study Your Teammates and the Opposition

As a quarterback in charge of running your team, you must know all its strengths and weaknesses. This means that you must make a study of the playing habits, abilities, and flaws of every player on your team.

In calling running plays, you must know the blocking abilities of your offensive linemen. One may be good at opening quick holes, but may not be able to hold off defensive linemen for more than a few seconds. Another may be slow in starting and unable to open a hole quickly. But once he does open the hole, he may be able to hold off a defender for as long as necessary.

Naturally your choice of running plays will be influenced by these factors.

Studying your backs is just as important. One runner may be a slow starter, but will have great power. Another may be extremely quick at starting, but may be much easier to knock off his feet. To get the best efforts out of each man, you must call your plays to take advantage of everybody's special abilities.

Your passing game will depend on how well you

know your receivers—the two ends and the half-backs. You must know the speed of each, as well as his ability to fake and to cut. And you must determine whether he catches passes with more confidence while running from left to right, or from right to left.

Whenever possible, use your teammates in plays where they feel most confident. This will increase their efficiency as individuals and will improve your offensive attack.

You must also study the opposition. Find out the weakness of each lineman. Learn which passing or running plays work well—and why. By talking to your coach and teammates, you will learn the weak spots in the enemy defense, and can choose plays which take advantage of those flaws.

Running with the Ball

There are two basic passing formations. The quarterback either stands in the "pocket," or "rolls out."

The pocket is an area in the backfield directly behind the center. The quarterback gets the ball and fades back to pass, with no trickery involved. His blockers line up in front of him in a rough semi-circle, protecting him against all rushing defensive players. The quarterback stands in the pocket, as you can see in the following diagram.

124

In "rolling out," the quarterback takes the ball from center and runs toward the sideline, behind a group of running blockers. He can pass the ball

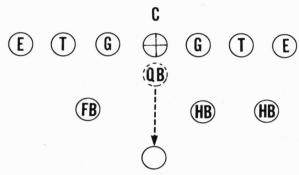

or, if he fails to spot a receiver, can run with it.

Whether a quarterback operates from the pocket or rolls out depends on the team's method of attack. Some teams vary their attack, using both formations.

In the roll-out style of play, the quarterback must be a good runner. Operating from the pocket requires no running ability at all.

The question of whether or not a quarterback *should* run with the football has been argued for years—and is still being argued.

Gary Wood, young quarterback for the New York Giants, likes to run, and gives his reasons below.

I'm convinced that being a good runner as well as a passer gives me a great advantage. Every time I take the ball and run toward the sidelines I'm keeping the defense "honest." By that I mean that they don't dare commit themselves too soon. If they charge at me and threaten to throw me for a loss, they know I'll throw the ball over their heads. If they drop back quickly to cover my receivers, they know I'll run. Knowing I have two weapons to choose from makes them hesitate. This helps my chances of being successful with either a run or a pass because they are forced to *react to my first move*. They are not able to take the initiative either by coming at me full speed (as if I were only a running back) or by covering my receivers (as if I were only a passer.)

Some NFL coaches don't like to have their quarterbacks run. They feel that their heavier running backs have a much better chance of gaining ground. A passer, on the other hand, can throw the ball more accurately while standing in the pocket.

Norm Van Brocklin, coach of the Minnesota Vikings, feels strongly that a quarterback should stay in the pocket.

I don't like to see a quarterback run unless he's unusually big and strong. Once a quarterback rolls out, he can really get hit hard—even harder than a running back—because he must *hesitate* while he runs. He has to look for openings to dash into, and at the same time be on the lookout for free receivers. Concentrating on so many things often prevents him from seeing a big defensive lineman coming right at him.

In the pocket, a passer has a much better chance of avoiding physical contact. Tacklers can't sneak up on him or hit him from behind. He has only to look in one direction—straight ahead—and the responsibility of controlling the defense is in the hands of his own linemen.

I breathe a lot easier when I see my quarterback standing in the pocket.

Your coach will have his own ideas about whether a quarterback should remain "protected" in the pocket, or roll out and therefore become a running as well as a passing threat.

All coaches do not agree, however, and your *next* coach may have different ideas. Therefore, you should learn both methods of passing. This will prevent your having to adjust to an entirely new style of play after you are graduated from school and begin to play under a new coach.

Protecting Yourself

Don't *ever* come to a dead stop after throwing a pass, no matter how you have thrown it or where you are standing.

If you are in the pocket, back up and duck your head behind your arms as soon as you let the ball go. Otherwise you will be helpless if a defensive player crashes into you. If you are on the run, *keep* running toward the sidelines after you have released the ball—until you are sure nobody is going to knock you down.

If you pass, but don't have time to avoid being tackled, then set yourself for the blow. Raise your arms quickly in front of your face and hold them there firmly. Your body can take more of a blow than your head.

Remember that in playing quarterback you must give equal emphasis to *all* the skills you have to develop. Don't spend hours practicing your passes because it's fun, and ignore fundamentals such as taking the ball from the center or handing off to the backs.

Just one flaw in your technique will greatly diminish your ability as a player.

Playing quarterback is a demanding job, for it requires just as much mental discipline as physical skill. There is no formula for any boy to become an outstanding quarterback. But if he is willing to practice hard at every little detail of play, he will gain control over his body, win the confidence of his teammates, and increase his chances of becoming outstanding in this key position.

Halfback

Halfbacks usually carry the ball on plays requiring quick starts or deception, rather than on "power plays" run straight through the line.

Halfbacks should be fast and shifty, able to accelerate quickly and change directions. They should have good body balance so that they can't be knocked off their feet easily. Sprinters, capable of running at great speed but unable to shift their weight quickly, won't make good halfbacks. Pure speed is only one factor in playing this position.

Passing ability is a valuable weapon for a halfback, for it lets him run the "option play." As he runs with the ball he has the choice of either running or passing, which makes him a double threat. If the defense knows he is likely to pass, they can't close in on him with confidence.

The ability to throw the ball can also keep a runner from being thrown for a loss when a running play backfires and he is trapped behind his line. He can heave the ball far downfield—making sure that it won't be intercepted. Even if the pass is not completed, he won't be tackled for a loss.

A halfback does not need great size. But he must be tough and durable, and big enough to block opposing linemen. Ideally, any running back should

129

have solidly built legs, for they are the source of his running power and his ability to shake off tacklers.

On an ordinary running play, the halfback may carry the ball, block for another runner, or serve as a decoy. (That is, he can fake taking a handoff and can run into the line.) On passing plays he may become a receiver or a decoy, or he may block for the passer.

To do his job as a runner, a halfback must start off with the proper stance. There are two basic stances —the two-point and the three-point stance—as you can see in the drawings opposite.

Most NFL coaches prefer their backs to use the three-point stance, because it forces the body to lean forward, assuring the runner of a faster start. It is the same type of starting position that trackmen use to get a quick spurt of speed when a race begins.

But the individual's body build must determine his choice. If the three-point stance doesn't feel comfortable, use the two-point stance.

Gripping the ball correctly while you run is very important. It not only prevents fumbles, but allows you to run faster than you will be able to if you hold

the ball in the wrong manner. The following drawing shows the proper grip.

Notice that the ball is *wedged* (rather than merely held) between your forearm and body. Your hand is cupped over the end of the football.

Although you should keep the ball close to your body at all times, cupping the ball allows you to *pump your arms* as you run. This will add to your speed. Holding the ball against your chest makes it impossible for you to travel with a natural stride, for it forces you to "waddle" from side to side. Hold-

ing the ball loosely, or away from your body, is inviting the opposition to "ball tackle" you by aiming their bodies at the ball rather than at you in the hope of making you fumble.

Using the proper stance, lean forward, ready to move. As soon as the center snaps the football, jump into action. If you delay, you will destroy the quarterback's timing in handing the ball off to you. He will be forced to halt his move and to hold the ball motionless. This will not only throw his timing off, but will tell the defense what play you are using.

If you start too quickly, on the other hand, you will be forced to slow down suddenly while you wait to get the ball from the quarterback. Not only will the timing of the play be ruined, but you will also lose body momentum and be much easier to tackle as you hit the line.

Although you must get a quick start as soon as the ball is snapped, *don't "take off" with the ball at full speed.* Most running backs, even in the NFL, cruise at only about eighty percent of their maximum speed until they find an opening in the line or a clear path to follow in the open field, where they can really use their speed.

Bill McPeak, coach of the Washington Redskins, feels that most young backs should avoid running at top speed the instant they get their hands on the ball. As he says:

When a boy is sprinting hard he loses the ability to fake, cut suddenly, or shift his weight. To avoid a tackler or a mass of players, a sprinting runner must suddenly jam on the brakes—and this means he loses body momentum.

It is much more sensible to hold a little speed in reserve and spurt ahead full force only when you see an opening.

Of course there are some runners who can take off at top speed with excellent balance and body control. One of these is our own great halfback, Charlie Taylor. At 215 pounds, Charlie has the speed of a sprinter, and is as light on his feet as a dancer.

But Charlie is an exception, and that's what makes him so great. The great majority of halfbacks should *not* sprint at full speed until they have broken through the line and are in an open field.

Running at a controlled rate lets you take advantage of the blocks thrown ahead of you. No matter which way a defensive man moves, you'll have a much better chance to avoid him if you're not running at full speed because you will be able to shift your direction quickly.

A halfback should develop ability as a pass receiver, for good halfbacks often serve as "third ends." Three good receivers running downfield are much more confusing to the defense than just two.

134

They can run more tricky pass patterns and put more pressure on defensive backs.

Taking the ball from the quarterback is a skill which *every* running back must perfect. You must learn to *take* the ball rather than *reach* for it. Reaching for the football slows you down, because extending your arms interferes with the smoothness of your natural stride. Let the quarterback *deliver* the ball to you. The only way to perfect this technique is to practice taking the ball from your quarterback again and again.

Fullback

PHYSICAL REQUIREMENTS

The fullback is the biggest back on the team. He must be big, strong, fairly fast (the faster the better, of course), and have powerful legs. He must be tough enough to block big defensive linemen, and very hard to knock off his feet. The fullback is the team's "bread and butter" runner. He must be able to pick up vital short yardage on bursts through the line in order to secure first downs.

The fullback uses the same basic techniques as those of a halfback in taking his stance, receiving the ball from the quarterback, holding the ball properly as he runs, and taking advantage of the first good opening he sees.

But on straight-ahead power plays, the fullback can start at full speed; he need not hold part of his speed in reserve. He won't be shifting his body, or suddenly cutting into a hole. On power plays he will simply run into the line, hoping his blockers will have opened a hole. Little deception is involved, except for the quarterback's faking a handoff to another runner, or fading back to "pass" after handing off the ball. Therefore, it would serve no purpose to hold speed in reserve.

FINE POINTS OF PLAY

Once the fullback breaks into the clear, he should take advantage of his blockers and become an "open-field runner," just like a halfback.

There is no sense in deliberately running into your opponents just to demonstrate your power. Even if you are big enough and strong enough to bowl them over, you will still be slowed down needlessly by the impact and will lose valuable steps in your race downfield.

Always make sure you grip the ball properly and firmly. On power plays a fullback often runs through a mass of players. Therefore he is more subject than a halfback to jolting tackles from all angles.

On power plays, the fullback should not get into the habit of "running blind,"—that is, putting his head down like a bull and charging into the line without even looking ahead. Often the hole he is supposed to go through never opens up. It would be foolish to ram blindly into a pile of players. An experienced player knows that he must slice into the line at a different angle.

If the hole you are running toward suddenly closes, *don't come to a dead stop.* Pivot or twist your body in a new direction, maintaining as much body momentum as possible, and plunge into the first opening you see. It is far better to make little or no gain than to be thrown for a loss.

Like any other player on the field, the fullback should study the moves of his opponents. He must learn the favorite tactics of each linebacker, and must pick out the linemen who offer good targets to run through. One defensive tackle may be a deadly tackler on straight-ahead power plays. But he may be a poor tackler on a play that is run past him at even a slight angle. The fullback should report all such observations to his quarterback.

A fullback must develop a "second effort." This means that as soon as he is hit, he instinctively keeps going, or plunges forward with all his power. This is more a matter of attitude than skill.

Blanton Collier, coach of the Cleveland Browns, has a fullback who always makes a second effort—the great Jimmy Brown. Says Blanton:

137

Time and time again I've seen Jimmy run into a pile of tacklers, and suddenly slow down as four men grab him. Every fan in the stands is sure that he has been stopped. But all of a sudden Jimmy will burst loose and charge down the field for more yardage.

Besides natural power and football instinct, Jimmy is blessed with the right attitude. He *thinks* good aggressive football. Being hit, or even slowed down to a crawl, doesn't mean that the play is over.

Jimmy puts every ounce of his great body power and leg drive into a second effort to break free. And he succeeds in doing so again and again. He never allows himself to think a play has ended until he hears the referee's whistle.

This is one reason why he is such a great fullback.

Holding the Ball for Place Kicking

PHYSICAL REQUIREMENTS

Usually a quarterback holds the ball for field-goal attempts, but any player on a team who has *excellent hand and finger control* can do the job.

FINE POINTS OF PLAY

The drawing on page 140 shows you the proper way to hold the ball for place kicks.

If the kicker is right-footed, the ball holder kneels on the kicker's right side, to allow him maximum leg room. He usually kneels on his right knee, holding his hands at knee height in front of his body. But this is not a strict rule. Some ball holders kneel on their left knee, and some on both knees, depending on which is more comfortable. Sometimes the ball holder's position is governed by the kicker's preference.

As the center spirals the ball, the holder catches it and quickly places it on the ground, nose down,

with both hands. Then, supporting the ball with his left hand, he places one finger of his right hand (either the middle or index finger) on top of the ball to hold it.

The ball should lean back slightly in the direction of the kicker, with the laces away from him toward the goal posts. This prevents the kicker's foot from hitting the laces and "spinning" the ball off to one side.

Once the ball is held firmly, the holder removes his left hand. With one finger of his right hand, he should press on the ball just hard enough to make sure it is locked in place, but not so hard that the pressure is liable to make it squirt from beneath his finger.

He must ignore the kicker, and *keep his eye right on the ball until it has been kicked* and is soaring through the air.

7
The Defensive Backfield

Linebacker

The three linebackers (right, left, and center) are involved in far more body contact than the other defensive backs (halfbacks and safeties). They must be big, strong, and fairly fast. But quick reactions are just as important as running speed. For in his position, from three to five yards behind the line, a linebacker has great responsibility.

He must be a deadly tackler. If he stops a runner, it will usually be for little or no gain. If he misses a tackle, the runner is often free to gain long yardage, especially when the deeper defensive backs are far downfield covering pass receivers.

A linebacker must be able to take consistent punishment, for he is in the thick of action on most running plays, and must absorb many hard blocks.

The three linebackers' jobs are not exactly alike. The center linebacker often "keys" on the opposing team's power runner, or fullback. He lines up opposite the runner, follows his moves to either side of the field, and is responsible for stopping him.

The left and right linebackers are responsible for running plays aimed in their direction. They must also be fast enough to race to their respective sidelines to back up the defensive end, if the end has been blocked out of a play in which the ball carrier is running wide.

A coach often plays his biggest, toughest linebacker at the center position, where he must make many head-on tackles in stopping power plays. Two lighter, faster players are better suited for the right and left positions, for they must be able to cover ends and backs attempting to catch short passes in their territory. (Although a short pass can also be thrown into the center linebacker's territory, he has less ground to cover since he is flanked on both sides by the other linebackers.)

There is no mystery to a linebacker's job of fighting off blockers and tackling the ball carrier. It calls for ruggedness and great determination.

But the hardest part of his job is to *quickly analyze the play the other team has called.* He must decide whether it will be a run or a pass; he must figure out who has the ball, and in which direction the play will travel.

If a linebacker is in the habit of rushing into the line too quickly, the opposing quarterback will call a fake run into the line and then calmly throw a short pass into the area the eager linebacker has just vacated. If the linebacker is overly cautious, and holds his position too long, he will be vulnerable to running plays. The quarterback will take advantage of his slowness in reaching the line.

No amount of raw ability, speed, or power can take the place of experience in becoming a good linebacker. If the offensive team has a smooth attack, there are many times when you simply *cannot* tell whether the quarterback is going to pass or hand the ball off, or which of two backs running into the line really has the ball.

A defensive back playing deeper in the defensive backfield doesn't have the same kind of pressure on him. He has more time to see what kind of play de-

145

velops before either a receiver or runner reaches his territory.

Besides tricky running plays, a linebacker must defend against two basic types of passes. One is the "quick slant," in which an end races two or three steps straight downfield, then quickly cuts behind the defensive line. If the linebacker has rushed up to the line to stop a running play, the end will be free to catch a short pass. The other passing technique is to have an end "delay." The end bumps a defensive lineman as if he is blocking for a running play. Then, when the linebacker charges toward the line, the end suddenly moves into the vacated area.

You can see that a linebacker has a rugged job. Not only must he guess whether the opposition is going to pass or run, but he is subject to the fakes of the quarterback, running backs, and ends.

As a result, he is often forced to gamble by making a strong move toward the area where he *thinks* a play will be aimed. Naturally he will sometimes be mistaken. But this should not discourage him, for even the greatest linebackers in the NFL sometimes make the wrong guess.

Vince Lombardi, coach of the Green Bay Packers, offers some helpful advice:

Any boy who wants to become a good linebacker must realize he has one of the toughest jobs on the

146

football field. He will have to try to stop a great variety of plays, and will be subject to many fakes by many players. As a result, it is impossible to be in the right place at the right time on every play.

Intelligent guessing based on experience is of great help in playing the position. You can develop this ability by being a keen observer of the opposition.

Study the moves of the quarterback to see if he "gives away" his intention of either passing or handing the ball to a runner. You'd be surprised at the way little mannerisms can tell you a great deal about opposing players. One quarterback may have the habit of unconsciously rubbing his hands together before taking the ball from center, if he is going to pass. Or he may glance quickly at the runner to whom he plans to hand the ball.

Apply the same "study technique" to backs and ends. Study their hands, the expression on their faces, or how they may tense their bodies nervously if they are going to be involved in the play.

Faking is another good weapon for a linebacker. *Be unpredictable.* Don't always make the same moves. Charge into the line at different angles. Or, if you don't actually intend to charge, fake a run by taking a couple of fast steps toward the line. Then quickly shuffle back to your normal depth just before the play begins. If you are constantly shifting and moving, you will keep the offense guessing.

This will balance the scales in terms of "pressure." The quarterback will be forced to react to *your* fakes, just as you must react to his.

Defensive Halfback

PHYSICAL REQUIREMENTS

Defensive halfbacks are usually lighter and faster than linebackers. They must be good tacklers in order to stop backs who have broken through the line and pass receivers who have caught the ball.

When stopping running plays, defensive halfbacks usually make tackles in a fairly open field, after a ball carrier is well on his way. As a result, they don't receive the same punishment from blockers as linebackers do.

Defensive halfbacks are responsible for more territory than linebackers, for they must cover pass receivers who run both shallow and deep. Linebackers, on the other hand, only cover the area a few yards behind the line of scrimmage.

Defensive halfbacks are key defenders in reacting to the tricky "option plays" run by quarterbacks or halfbacks. In such plays the runner can either pass or throw. If a defensive halfback guesses wrong and makes a bad move, the opposition may

148

gain much yardage. On deep passing plays, he must call upon quick reactions and great speed to prevent receivers from breaking into the clear.

Although a defensive halfback may not even get near the football for three or four plays in a row, he may have *total defensive responsibility* on the next play. Just one wrong step in covering an enemy pass receiver can result in a touchdown. For often the halfback is solely responsible for stopping one of the most dramatic plays in football, the "bomb"— a long pass intended to score a touchdown.

Sometimes a defensive halfback's job can be man-to-man coverage of a deep receiver.

FINE POINTS OF PLAY

In making tackles, a defensive halfback will usually face ball carriers in an open field. He should not charge a runner directly, but should use *feints* to "cut him off," forcing the runner toward one side of the field. This will give other defensive players a good chance to catch the runner. (Remember the methods of "dueling" with a runner as discussed in the section on tackling.)

Covering pass receivers is a very exacting job. If possible, take away *two* routes from a receiver as he speeds downfield, and allow him only *one*. For example, if he is slicing across the field toward one sideline, remain half a step behind him and to his outside (between him and your goal line). Keep close to him, as in the following diagram.

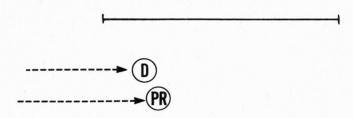

This takes away his ability to cut sharply. If he tries to cut downfield he will bump into you. This will result in an "offensive interference" penalty being called against his team. To go deep downfield, he must suddenly slow down and cut behind you. This will make him lose so much speed that he will have to start running a new pass pattern, which will confuse his quarterback. In other words, it is possible to limit a pass receiver's routes by clever positioning of your body.

If a receiver does get free, don't always make a "do-or-die" effort to intercept or knock down the pass. Each play must be judged according to its own importance and according to the size of the gamble you would be taking.

On a very short pass, give the end the completion. Don't think you must rush in and try to make an interception, especially if it is a sideline pass, where you and the receiver are all alone. You might intercept the pass or knock the ball down. But if you miss, the receiver is free to catch the pass and run down the sidelines—often for a touchdown. In this situation, it is more sensible to give away five yards than to take a fifty-fifty chance of giving away a touchdown.

This doesn't mean that you should stand by helplessly and watch every short pass be completed. But before trying for an interception, *calculate carefully*. Make sure you are close enough to the receiver to make your move. You have only an instant to dart between the passer and the receiver —and that instant must be when the ball is in the air. If a passer fakes a throw with his arm and you leap forward, you will have made a deadly mistake. The receiver will dash down the field past you and be in the clear for an easy pass.

The longer a pass, the more time a defensive back has to jump in between the passer and the receiver while the ball is in the air. There are no rules to determine how far a pass must travel before you should try for an interception. It is a matter of judging your receiver and his speed, your own position in relation to him, and the speed with which the quarterback throws the ball. If the quarterback isn't smart enough to fake with his arm before actually passing, or *must* throw quickly because he is about to be tackled, your job will be much easier.

On a "fly" pattern (when a fast receiver dashes straight down the field, trying to use sheer speed to get past his defender) don't try to remain in front of the receiver unless you know that the safety plans to stay behind him, allowing you to "double-team" the receiver by staying in front of him. The secret of covering such a deep receiver all by yourself is to *remain one step behind him*—contrary to the popular but wrong idea that you should never let a receiver get ahead of you. While a step behind your man, you will only have to look straight ahead to see him. And there will be only one angle at which a pass can be completed: straight over your head and right into his arms. In other words, you can be "beaten" only by a perfect pass.

If you make the mistake of staying in front of a fast receiver, you won't be able to run freely, because you will have to keep looking back over your shoulder to see where he is. Since you will not have good body balance, he can easily "shake" you by suddenly cutting to one side.

Paul Krause, great young defensive halfback of

the Washington Redskins, knows that he must always watch the receiver's head—and must always remain one step behind the receiver. For no matter how many fakes the receiver makes with his body, he can't catch the ball until he looks back over his shoulder to see it coming through the air.

If you are "beaten" on a deep pass play, don't make the mistake of thinking you have failed, and change your style of play. All a defensive back can do is to try his very hardest. Your coach won't expect anything more from you.

Don't forget that every time a touchdown pass is thrown in the NFL, a great defensive back like Paul has been scored on.

Safety

PHYSICAL REQUIREMENTS

Since the two safeties play the deepest defensive positions on the field, they form the "last line of defense." This means that they must be sure, deadly tacklers and excellent pass defenders. Since they often stand alone between an opposing runner or pass receiver and their own goal line, they have great responsibility.

By playing deeper than defensive halfbacks,

safeties have more time to cover deep receivers. But unfortunately, tricky receivers also have more time to fool the safeties and break into the clear to catch a pass. Therefore, a safety must have exceptional speed to catch up with, or remain close to, a pass receiver.

Besides covering pass receivers, the safety sometimes has to come rushing upfield, toward the line of scrimmage, to stop a running play. But they usually make fewer tackles than halfbacks. The safety will be involved only when a runner breaks away for a fairly good gain. (On short-yardage gains, defensive linemen or linebackers make the tackle and on medium-sized gains, the linebackers or halfbacks stop the runner.)

Safeties do not have to be big, or able to take great punishment, for by the time a ball carrier reaches their territory he is in the open field, and will try to use feints rather than knock tacklers over.

FINE POINTS OF PLAY

The safety's job is not very different from that of a defensive halfback, except that he is called upon to make fewer tackles, and is more often engaged in a "goal-line duel" with deep pass receivers.

But the safety does not operate as an isolated

player with a single, specific job. Each safety must *coördinate* his efforts with other players, especially the defensive halfback who plays in front of him. Because he stands behind every other member of his team, the safety is the only player with a *total view* of the field. He is better able to sense the nature of a play, or the direction it will take, since he has more time to size up the fakes of the opposition, and the action will take longer to reach his area of play.

If a ball carrier has burst through the line, the safety immediately moves upfield in a position to stop him. But he *doesn't* charge at the runner directly. Instead, he watches his halfback approach the runner and force him to one side. Then he makes his own move. In other words, he lets the halfback cut off the runner, forcing him toward a sideline, and then moves in to help with the tackle.

If, on the other hand, he sees his halfback playing a very aggressive role and charging a runner at full speed, he will wait before making his own move because the halfback will probably either tackle the runner or miss him completely. As a result, the safety must remain behind the halfback in order to make the tackle if the halfback fails to do so.

The safety must always plan his moves to take

advantage of the defensive halfback's judgment and ability—both on running and passing plays.

A safety must also make plans with the halfback to coördinate their efforts in covering dangerous pass receivers. For example, if a very tricky, fast receiver comes downfield, both the safety and defensive halfback must know exactly what they are going to do. If the safety agrees to keep behind the receiver (between him and the goal line), the halfback will be free to gamble, by remaining close to the receiver and trying for an interception. If he misses, the safety will be backing him up to stop the receiver after he catches the pass.

If they hadn't planned such a move, the defensive halfback might be forced to "play it safe" by not taking the chance of making an interception. As a result, he would probably allow a fairly short pass to such a dangerous receiver to be completed.

On most school teams, both safeties do the same job. They play deep, coöperate with other defensive backs in covering pass receivers, and make tackles when necessary.

But in the NFL, most teams use one safety as a "free safety." He is usually a very experienced defensive back who has excellent speed and timing. He also has good football instinct, which lets him "smell out" enemy pass plays. Rather than being assigned to a specific area or to a specific pass receiver (as are the other defensive backs), he is allowed to roam free. He uses his judgment and guesswork to charge all over the field, speeding into areas where he feels a pass will be thrown, and trying for interceptions. This style of defensive play naturally calls for other defensive backs to "cover" the area he leaves unguarded.

Nate Ramsey, the young safety of the Philadelphia Eagles, knows he must remain alert to avoid making a common mistake.

If an offense depends primarily on a running attack, and throws only an occasional short pass, the defensive safeties may spend most of the game merely standing in place and watching the action. This may tempt the safeties to become relaxed and careless. Don't make the mistake of thinking a play has ended just because you see a mass of tacklers swarm over the opposing quarterback, who is trying to pass, or because you see a runner "stopped" by what looks like a sure tackle.

The passer can "miraculously" dodge from beneath the tacklers and suddenly throw a pass. Or the runner can burst loose with a great second effort. If you have not done your job by moving into the proper defensive position, you may be forced to watch helplessly as the quarterback throws a long pass over your head to a receiver who has sneaked behind you into the end zone. Or the "trapped" ball carrier may outrace you and score a touchdown just because you were careless.

Make it a rule to stay on your toes until you hear the whistle which officially ends every play.

8
Football in the NFL

School football teams play under many different rules and systems, depending on the size of the school, its geographical location, and the policies of the team's coach.

But football in the NFL is a highly skilled game with its own set of rules and playing techniques. By learning more about this style of play, you will increase your understanding of the game. In addition, you will get much more pleasure from watching exciting NFL action on the field.

Following are diagrams of the basic offensive formations used in the NFL, simple explanations of "specialized positions" on a team, and basic descriptive terms used by players and coaches.

Specialized Positions

The flanker back is one of the two offensive half-backs used in the T formation. Instead of lining up in a "deep" position so he can run with the ball, he takes his position just behind the line of scrimmage, often to the outside of one end. The flanker is most often used to catch passes; he gives a pro team three quick-starting receivers.

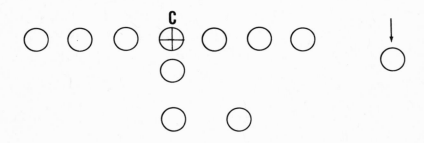

FREE SAFETY

The free safety is an experienced, smart defensive safety who is allowed to "roam free" rather than being given a specific assignment. He runs all over the field, wherever he senses the action will take place, trying to break up pass plays.

Most pro teams line up with one split end, a fast light receiver, and a tight end. The tight end plays tightly against the tackle, close to the line. Besides being able to catch passes, he is usually far bigger and stronger than most pass-catching ends, and he does a lot of blocking.

Offensive Formations

DOUBLE WING

As you can see, both ends are split, and both halfbacks (the "double wings") also play wide. This is a good passing formation, for it puts both ends and both halfbacks in a position to get a fast start into enemy territory.

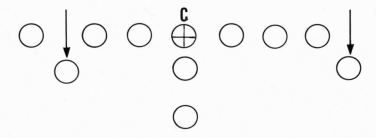

Notice that this is even more of an extremely "spread-out" formation, and is also suited to a passing game.

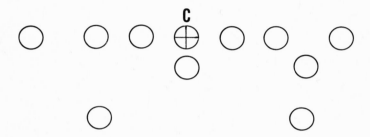

The "back" referred to is the halfback. The "slot" he is filling is the position between the end and the tackle, caused by the end "splitting," or moving away from the line of scrimmage.

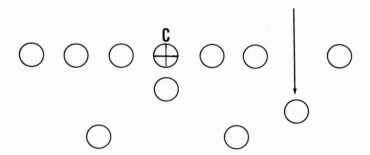

The quarterback plays deep, and the other backs are widely spread. This is primarily a passing offense.

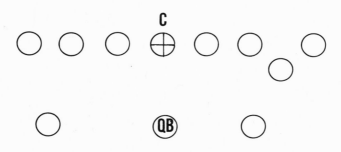

Descriptive Terms

AUTOMATIC

An optional change of play which the quarterback calls in the huddle. He arranges for a key phrase to be called when the team lines up, ready to move into action. The quarterback calls this key phrase just before he takes the ball from center, if he is convinced the defense is so arranged that they would stop the original play.

BOOTLEG

A sneak run by the quarterback, who fakes a handoff, then runs around end alone, with the ball hidden against his hip.

BUTTON-HOOK

A pass-catching move in which the receiver dashes down the field, then suddenly circles back sharply to face the passer as he receives the ball.

CLIPPING (A PENALTY)

An illegal block from the rear, in which a player is blocked across the back of his leg.

COFFIN CORNER

The area bounded by the goal line and the side-line. A punt that goes out of bounds in this area—usually inside the ten-yard line—is called a "coffin corner kick," for it pins the other team deep in its own territory.

COUNTER

A tricky running play in which a back runs into the line in an opposite direction to his team's original flow of movement.

FAIR CATCH

A "compromise" made by a player about to

catch a punt. By raising his arm straight up in the air, he promises not to run with the ball. But at the same time he is not allowed to be tackled. The ball is placed down where he catches it.

FLY

A pass pattern in which the receiver takes off straight down the field in an effort to get clear, deep in enemy territory.

MONSTER

A "floating" linebacker, who tries to confuse the opposition by varying his position and methods of attack from play to play.

NAKED REVERSE

After one ball carrier runs behind a wall of blockers, he hands the ball to another back, who runs in the other direction without a single blocker in front of him.

OPTION PLAY

When a quarterback or halfback has the option, or choice, of running with the ball or passing it. Usually he makes up his mind according to how the defense reacts to his moves.

ROLL OUT

The quarterback takes the ball and runs wide, ready to run or pass as he sees fit.

SPLIT END

An offensive end is positioned a few yards wide of his line. This enables him to avoid the jarring body contact of line play, and to get a faster start downfield.

ZONE BLOCK

A block used against tricky, shifting defenses which try to fool the offense. The blocker is not sent against a specific defender; instead, he simply blocks the man nearest him as he charges forward.

Index

170

About the Author

RICHARD PICKENS is the editor–author of *The NFL Guide to Physical Fitness,* also published by Random House. A graduate of Bowdoin College, he played both football and baseball while in school. Since graduation he has worked as a television editor and a free-lance writer. His feature articles and interviews have been syndicated in newspapers throughout the country and in Europe.

Mr. Pickens is married, and lives in New York City.